THE
MESSAGE
AND ITS
MESSENGERS

THE
MESSAGE
AND ITS
MESSENGERS

Daniel T. Niles

Prepared for the Board of Missions
of The Methodist Church

Published by Abingdon Press
NEW YORK   NASHVILLE

THE MESSAGE AND ITS MESSENGERS

Copyright © 1966 by Abingdon Press

Library of Congress Catalog Card Number: 66-10922

SET UP, PRINTED, AND BOUND BY THE
PARTHENON   PRESS,   AT   NASHVILLE,
TENNESSEE, UNITED STATES OF AMERICA

TO
JOHN COVENTRY SMITH
ALFORD CARLETON
EUGENE L. SMITH

PREFACE

THIS BOOK IS BASED ON A SERIES OF LECTURES DELIVERED AT A METH-odist consultation on the Christian Mission. I have asked Dr. Tracey Jones to say, in a foreword, something about this consultation and the place of these lectures in it. I am grateful that Abingdon Press felt that these lectures could have a wider circulation and undertook to publish them.

When I prepared these lectures I did not hesitate to incorporate in them material which appears in various books of mine; so that when the question of publishing them arose, I had to decide what to do about this material. I have decided to leave it as it is without any attempt to show where, in my other books, it appears. This material is an integral part of the lectures and is in no sense "quoted matter."

Naturally, I have edited the lectures. It was necessary to make the presentation tighter, to eliminate repetition, and to make the style appropriate to what has to be read and not just heard. But these remain lectures nevertheless and retain, I hope, something of the thrust of the spoken word. Only in a few instances have I allowed the direct reference to Methodism and Methodists to remain.

7

It can well be asked what purpose such a book as this will serve—a book in which there is no developing argument and where seemingly unrelated themes are dealt with in succession. The answer must be that a discussion concerning the Christian Mission must take into account a whole developing history and the many concerns which that history points up.

While casually glancing through a magazine, on a plane traveling from London to Colombo, I came across a poem which struck me greatly. A quote from it is printed after this preface. The lines of this poem had kept running through my mind as I prepared these lectures. They seemed to say: "Look at the Church. Is she not like that mill?" These lectures are an attempt to say that she is and that she is not and that she need not be. The river that turned the mill is still there and flowing in force, though no mill will do either for today or tomorrow. The mill is yesterday's proof of the power that is there, even though its mediation of that power is no longer sufficient today nor will it be able to mediate that power any more tomorrow.

I have dedicated the book to three men, to each of whom I owe a great deal both in personal friendship and in understanding of what it means to engage in the Christian mission. It is also my tribute to them for all that their leadership has meant to the cause of Christian missions.

DANIEL T. NILES

THE MILL

No one lives there now, except
The rabbits

. . . .
The stream, weed choked where once it swept
The old wheel round, . . .
Can only gently creak the sluice gate chain.
New sedge grass grows where once the water churned,
And brambles bind the stones which crushed the grain.

No one works there any more,

. . . .
        Ivy locks the hingeless door
The rotting wheel, . . .
        no longer feels the weight
Of torrents. Water ruled its frame before,
Now stagnant pools replace the former spate.[1]

              TONY ULOTH

[1] *Country Life,* April 25, 1963. Used by permission of the author.

FOREWORD

THE CHAPTERS IN THIS BOOK BY
D. T. NILES ARE THE LECTURES
that he gave to 140 Methodist leaders from 30 countries
who met at Gatlinburg, Tennessee, in April, 1964.
When one reads the reports of the working committees
of that consultation, one can recognize the impact that
these lectures had. This should be no surprise. For the
past twenty-five years the creative mind, the masterful
use of the English language, and the Christian insight
of D. T. Niles have been felt throughout the Christian
world. This book provides invaluable help to Christians facing a world in which the missionary movement
begins where a man of faith in Christ meets a person
who has no such faith, where the mission field includes
all six continents, and where the time for change in
program and organization has come.

The Gatlinburg Consultation was preceded by three
regional Methodist meetings. In 1961 the first of the
three was held in the Congo. Seventy leaders from
Liberia, Rhodesia, Mozambique, the Republic of South
Africa, and the Congo were present. The freedom of
the African churches to determine their own life was
the dominant theme.

In February, 1962, the second consultation was held
in Buenos Aires, Argentina. Ten Latin American

11

countries, including Cuba, had representatives present. Two priorities came to the surface. The first was the need of the churches in Latin America to be more aware of and involved in social change. The second was the sense of urgency felt by Latin American Protestant leaders that the local congregation, organized into small cell groups, would provide the most relevant form of missionary structure for the churches.

The third regional meeting was convened at Port Dickson, Malaysia, in November, 1963. At this consultation there were men and women from Pakistan, India, Malaysia, Indonesia, the Philippines, Hong Kong, Taiwan, Korea, Okinawa, and Japan. Much to the surprise of everyone, the idea that loomed above all others was the conviction that the time had come for the churches in Asia to move toward autonomy.

The Gatlinburg Consultation was an attempt to bring together these many and varied themes. As was true in the regional meetings, the purpose was neither legislative nor to plan for the future. Rather it presented an opportunity to define in a world perspective the nature of the challenges and possibilities facing the churches throughout the world. Dr. Niles was asked to provide this leadership. He flew to Tennessee from Ceylon to give these lectures and then immediately returned to Asia. These chapters, therefore, can best be understood when they are seen as an effort to help church leaders from five continents face the challenges of our day and to find, within both the biblical world and contemporary history, guidelines from God as to what he requires of his Church.

Tracey K. Jones, Jr.
Associate General Secretary, World Division
Board of Missions of The Methodist Church

CONTENTS

1. WHENCE?
WHENCE IS
OUR ASSURANCE? 17

2. WHAT?
WHAT IS OUR TASK? 33

3. HOW?
HOW SHALL WE
DO OUR WORK? 47

4. WHERE?
WHERE DO OUR
TEMPTATIONS LIE? 61

5. WHEN?
WHEN IS THE CHURCH
THE CHURCH? 89

6. WHY?
WHY DIVIDE OUR
HERITAGE? 107

7. WHITHER?
WHITHER ARE
WE BOUND? 120

CHAPTER 1
WHENCE IS OUR ASSURANCE?

What I shall attempt in this first chapter will be in the nature of a biblical introduction. The purpose of this book is to look at the Church, or that part of it to which we belong, and to ask questions about its faith, its mission, its structure, and its direction for the future.

Let me begin with a story, an incident that took place at the Assembly of the World Council of Churches at Evanston in 1954. It was the night when Archbishop Michael of the Orthodox Church was speaking about the Church. For the first half hour, as one listened to him, one knew he was describing the Church as it is talked about in the Bible—the Church as the Body of Christ and the Bride of Christ. But all of a sudden, without any warning, we discovered that he was talking about the Orthodox Church. Angus Dun, the Episcopal Bishop of Washington at that time, who was sitting next to me at the meeting, tapped me on the knee and said, "D. T., she'll be coming 'round the mountain when she comes."

This happens not only when one is talking about the Orthodox Church but when one is talking about any church. When we hear someone talking about the Church, we think, in our own minds, that they are talking about our church. Those of us who have studied in theological colleges, along with men of other denominations, know this experience. One goes to one's class in theology, and the professor is talking about the Church. I think that he is talking about the Methodist Church, the Presbyterian next to me thinks that he is talking about the Presbyterian Church, and the Lutheran next to him thinks that he is talking about the Lutheran Church; and for all of us, "She'll be coming 'round the mountain when she comes."

There is somehow a gulf! And there is no way that we know of bridging that gulf between the Church, as we confess the Church when we say, "I believe in the Holy Catholic Church," and that particular church to which you or I belong.

In *Great Expectations,* by Charles Dickens, there is a description of Miss Havisham as Pip first saw her. She was sitting by a gilded looking glass, dressed as she had been dressed for what was to have been her wedding day. Jewels sparkled on her neck and on her hands. She was wearing rich materials—satins and lace and silks; and a long veil hung from her hair. But everything which ought to have been white had been white long since and was now faded and yellow, while the bride within the bridal dress had withered like the dress and like the flowers; and all the clocks had stopped at twenty minutes to nine.

That may well serve as a picture of the Church as many see the Church today. It is well to remind ourselves of this, so that we may remember what our task is. Our primary task is to ask God to tell us how we, in our day and generation, and in the places where God has put us, can so enter into the reality of the Church that those who see us can see in us and through us and by us the Church made visible—visible in its beauty, visible in its freshness, visible as the bride and body of Christ. We do not change the Church. It is the Bride of Christ, the Body of Christ. All we can do and must do is to make that Church visible, a little more visible, that men may see it in its beauty and its power. In other words, there is a stern restriction on what we are allowed to do. We are not allowed, and we cannot believe that we shall be allowed, to change the Church. And, because we are not allowed to change it in our attempt to make it visible, we are not free.

Let me illustrate this. I remember the day when we were celebrating in Ceylon the formation of the Church of South India. The coming into being of the Church of South India was, on the one hand, an event wherein churches united; while, on the other hand, it was an event through which churches which had been dependent on church missionary societies became free. One of the men who brought greetings on that occasion said in his speech: "The Church is never free; it is bound. It is bound by the will of its Lord, it is bound by its nature, and you cannot do with it what you like."

I think we shall all discover that there is a limit to our own freedom—our freedom of discussion and our

freedom of decision. The limits are given to us by the
nature of the Church and its Lord. In this first chapter,
therefore, I have decided to look at the nature of the
faith which we confess, the faith which sets us our
tasks; and for this purpose I have chosen one passage,
the eighth chapter of the book of Romans, as our
guiding text.

I have found it very useful, especially when dealing
with general themes, to restrict myself to a particular
passage of Scripture and not go from one verse to another. When one is doing that, one is always in a sense
free somehow to set up one's own pattern of argument.
But when one is bound by a passage, the argument is
fixed. Here is one way in which the preacher can de-
liver himself from himself. It is a deliverance that all
of us preachers want; for a preacher, when he gets into
the pulpit, must find some method by which he avoids
the temptation to take the argument the way he wants
it to go.

There are five verbs which together describe the
Christian response to the gospel—I *believe,* I *hope,* I
love, I *obey,* I *know.* Because, in his letter to the
Corinthians, Paul has the first three verbs together,
somehow those three verbs are often considered to come
first. But let us not forget the other two—I *obey,* I
know. In Romans 8, the emphasis is on the verb *know;*
and perhaps it is well that we begin with a verb on
which John Wesley insisted so much. Whence is the
assurance of Christian knowledge? What is it that we

know, that we are certain about? What are the certainties under which we live, the certainties by which we are delivered, the certainties to which we are bound? In this eighth chapter of his letter to the Romans, Paul works to the climax of an argument which he begins in the first chapter at the end of the preface. The preface end with the words, "The righteousness of God is revealed." Then the argument begins with the words, "For the wrath of God is revealed." These two are set side by side in the seventeenth and the eighteenth verses of the first chapter. "The righteousness of God is revealed"—that is the gospel. "The wrath of God is revealed"—that is the situation. The two things belong to each other.

G. K. Chesterton, in his book *Orthodoxy,* has an argument about the irrationality of the Christian faith. He talks about a key. Suppose you take a key, he says—there is no point in arguing as to whether that key is logically constructed, or whether it is esthetically constructed. Obviously, that key can be made any way one likes and made very beautifully. But the important point about the key is simply this, Does it fit the lock? The logic of the key is the logic of the lock. The logic of the righteousness that is revealed is the logic of the wrath that is revealed. This is something that is true about our world, and it is that truth which the truth of the gospel unlocks. And both truths belong to God. It is this argument of the relationship between the righteousness that is revealed in the gospel and the wrath of God that is revealed in the world—the correlation between those two—which Paul works out in great detail in the first seven chapters.

Let me use an illustration from our Lord himself. We remember his saying, "He that does not gather with me scatters" (Luke 11:23). Sometimes on a Saturday I spend the day dusting my library. I take the books from the shelves, dust them, and put them back. When my son was quite small, he would come to me and say, "Papa, I want to help." So I would show him a shelf and say, "All right, you go and dust that one." He would pull down all the books, get a rag and dust the shelf, and put all the books back again. He would then come to me and say, "I have done it." So I would say, "Very good, now you go and play." And after he was gone, I would have to do it all over again because all the books were in the wrong places and the shelf had not been dusted properly anyway. He thought he was helping me but he wasn't.

You cannot just help God. That is why Jesus says, "Unless you are actually gathering with me, even though you think you are gathering, you are scattering." We think, for instance, that we are building peace; but there is only one way of building peace, and that is the way in which God builds it himself. We are living in a world in which God himself is at work, and what God is doing determines the grain of the universe. If you are working on a piece of wood, you must work according to the grain; otherwise, you will only get splinters. We are not free. There is a grain in the universe; there is a grain in history; there is a grain in the Church, because God is at work. And if we do not gather with him, however wonderful our plans, however ardently we labor, however carefully we work, the result of it all is scattering, not gathering.

As we look at the world in which we are living, to use another picture, it is a world where the tides are running high. In our national life in Asia, the tides in every country are running high. The same is true in Africa and in South America. In the United States of America, too, the tides are running high. Everywhere public issues have entered into the private lives of men. To use a phrase of George Eliot, there is "the invasion of our private lives by the larger destinies of mankind." I remember a lecture by John R. Mott in which he said, "When the tide is running high you want expert pilots, pilots who know how to navigate the ship and bring it to harbor." We cannot control the tide, but we have got to navigate the ship. We cannot decide the grain, but we have got to work with this piece of wood. "The wrath of God is revealed. The righteousness of God is revealed." Here are the ultimate limits of man's freedom.

We notice how, in the eighth chapter, Paul comes right down to the first person. When he comes to talk about the certainties of our faith, he is talking about the certainties of my faith, of your faith, of each man's faith. There are many reasons for that, but there is one reason which it may be right to remember at this point. Let me put it this way: It is our purpose to decide issues about the Church, the Methodist Church; but ultimately the only issues we can decide are issues about ourselves. The Church is not at my mercy or yours. Tracey Jones has said, "The final decisions are Christ's, but the intermediate skirmishes are dependent on us." That is true; but the way we deal with these intermediate skirmishes does not decide the final verdict about the issues, it does decide the final verdict about ourselves. We are going to do things which concern our eternal destiny as people, because we are called to deal with the question of obedience, obedience to the nature of the Church, obedience to the nature of the faith.

Have you not been intrigued by the fact that when you read Paul you find there an interesting fact, that whenever he is thinking about himself and his salvation, he is again and again in doubt? "I buffet my body and bring it under bondage, lest having preached to others I myself should be damned." (I Cor. 10:27.) But when he is talking about his calling to be an apostle to the Gentiles, he does not seem to be in doubt. In other words, Paul is quite sure what God has asked him to do; only he is not at all sure what is going to happen to him. That is the only kind of attitude which will help us to ask and to receive the answer to the question, What does God want us to do?

In the preface that J. B. Phillips has written to his paraphrase of the New Testament, he says, "Again and again the writer felt rather like an electrician rewiring an ancient house without being able to turn the mains off." We know how hazardous such an operation can be; and yet that is the kind of operation which we are being called upon to undertake. With what attitude of mind and spirit shall we undertake it? I think a look at this eighth chapter of Romans may help put our souls, our minds, and our spirits into the kind of attitude with which we can enter into this task.

First of all, the eighth chapter of Romans opens with a *now!* "There is therefore *now* no condemnation for those who are in Christ Jesus, for the law of the spirit of life in Christ Jesus has set me free from the law of sin and death." It is not that it has set me free from sin; it has set me free from the law of sin. Paul works up to the climax of his argument in the seventh chapter, when he comes out with that agonizing cry, "Oh, wretched man that I am." And then there is the answer, "Thank God through Jesus Christ." What has God done? God has changed the law. Under the law which demanded obedience I am guilty; but now the law does not demand obedience, it demands faith. Under that law I am not guilty. We remember that incident in the life of Peter when Jesus says to him, "Peter, the devil has asked permission to sift you, but I have prayed for you that your faith fail not." Was that prayer answered? Of course it was. Peter denied his Lord, but his faith did not fail; and because his faith did not fail, he ultimately found repentance and renewal.

"We now stand under a new law"—that is the first certainty. What God demands of me is faith, the willingness to trust myself in his hands and to leave myself there even when I do not trust him. What does that mean? When we study the book of Psalms, again and again we find the psalmist in a mood of quarreling with God, finding fault with God, arguing with God. The psalmist seems to take liberties with God which we do not take. It is a good thing to be able to do that. If you cannot scold God when life goes wrong, whom else can you scold?

I sometimes like to put it to myself like this. We must learn to know God not only as father but also as mother. When things go wrong in the house, maybe we do not like to grumble against father, but we would like to grumble against mother. There is a sense in which there is a closeness between mother and child which does not exist between father and child. And the psalmist seems to know how to treat God as mother— to go to God and say: "You had no business to do this." "Why did you do this?" "I am angry because you did this." But it is to God that the psalmist goes and to whom he speaks. Faith is to trust oneself in God's hands even when one has lost faith—to leave oneself there, to be in mother's arms. The child yells if it wants to yell, but still it is in its mother's arms. That is the situation which Paul says has been created for us in the gospel; and this is made effectual by the Holy Spirit which teaches us to say, "My Father."

When I was a student at the university, I believed what I had read in so many books, that the fatherhood of God and the brotherhood of man were common teaching in the various religions—until we had the experience once as a group of Christian students having a conference with a Hindu. It was a three-day conference, and its program was that we Christians took this practicing, pious Hindu friend with us, sat with him, and tried to tell him what Christianity was, and sought to find out what he had to say. Every time we told him something, he smiled and nodded his head and said, "Yes, I believe that." For two days we were telling him about Christianity and he believed everything we said, but still he was a Hindu. We were getting madder and madder because we could not find something he did not believe, until somebody said, "God is Father." He shook his head and said, "I don't believe that." We had at last discovered what he didn't believe.

The truth that God is Father is what you will not find in any other religion except Christianity. No wonder Paul says, "Nobody has ever learned to call God Father except in and through the Holy Spirit." The Holy Spirit teaches me to call God Father, to believe that God thinks of me as me. And then Paul goes on: In order to come to this experience I don't have to be a particular kind of person, because this is for all creation. At the end of the eleventh chapter, where this discussion ends, Paul closes with those glorious words: "For of him, and through him, and to him, are all things." All things and, therefore, I also. Or, to use the words of Charles Wesley, "So wide it passed by none, or it had passed by me." The mercy of God is so wide, the grace of God is so wide, that it did not pass anyone by. That is why I know that it did not pass me by. I was the last on the list.

Where is the ground of our certainty that you and I are within God's grace? Paul would say, "The ground of my certainty that I am included is that nobody is excluded"—the whole creation, everything, all things. But this does not mean that you or I can take God's grace for granted. Paul goes on: "I can take this, I can inherit this, I can make this my own and live by it only through a life of prayer." But here again, the certainty by which I live is that God does not answer *my* prayers. Rather, God answers the prayers of the Holy Spirit praying in me. If God should simply answer my prayers or yours, we should be sunk. It is a great thing that God does not answer our prayers, because we do not know how to pray, we do not know what to pray about, we do not know what to pray for. We pray all wrong, just as that lame man in the temple who, when he saw Peter and John, stretched out his hand and said, "I want some alms." Peter said to him: "You don't want alms. What are alms for? What you want is to stand up and walk." (Acts 3:1-6.) He had been sitting at that temple door so long asking for the wrong thing that he had forgotten to ask for the right thing. Most of us are in that position. But, thank God, says Paul, "God listens to the prayers of the Holy Spirit."

Yes, we are praying that God's will may be done. But mixed up in those prayers that we are praying will be our own ideas, our own convictions, our own opinions, our own prejudices, and everything else. But thank God, he will not answer those prayers. He answers the prayers of the Holy Spirit, who teaches us to pray through grace.

At this point, there is a swing in the eighth chapter from the individual to the whole, just as earlier there was a swing from the whole to the individual. "We know," says Paul, "that in everything God works for good; for those whom he foreknew he also predestined." This truth about predestination is a very difficult truth to understand, nor do I intend to deal with it at length. But it is important. Let us forget Paul's method of argument for the moment and look at this truth through a figure. It is the destination of all things that is fixed. What we are talking about is predestination, not predestiny. In other words, if you get inside a train in New York and you are going to Boston, the destination of that train is fixed. It is going to Boston. But what happens inside the train is not fixed. You may get a companion who is dead drunk. If you were in Ceylon, you might get bitten by bugs. All kinds of things can happen in the train. Your

destiny is not fixed but your destination is. And Paul
makes it quite clear that the destination of everything
is fixed. Everything is going to Jesus Christ. There is
nowhere else to go. How do I know that when I die I
will go to Jesus Christ? Because that is where everything and everybody goes. That is the destination.

But, while it is true that the destination is fixed, and
while it is true that everyone is on that train and cannot get out, since there is nowhere else to go, it is not
true that you or I will necessarily be allowed either to
drive the engine or be the guard. Those people have to
be chosen, elected. Some are chosen, others are not.
Jacob is chosen; Esau is not chosen. Abel is chosen;
Cain is not chosen. Abraham is chosen; Lot is not
chosen. For what? For driving the train. As bearers of
the gospel in history, God chooses some and does not
choose others. He has chosen us. Why? Only God
knows. If you or I were God, and we wanted to win
this world for Jesus Christ, is this the group we would
choose? I am sure not. But God chose us. Scripture
simply says that we do not know why.

But that does not mean, Paul would go on, that
those who are the bearers of the gospel are the people
who will ultimately populate heaven. We must get
those two ideas separated. I may be a bearer of the
gospel but I shall not necessarily be there. "Everybody
talking about heaven ain't going there." To continue
with the analogy we have been using, simply because
we are on the train and the train's destination is fixed

does not mean that when we get off the train we can go home. There is a ticket collector at the other end. The doctrine of predestination, the doctrine of election, and the doctrine of the last judgment must be held together. That we shall go to Jesus Christ is true because he is our judge.

So are we left with those certainties out of which we must work, think, and decide—certainties that restrict our area of freedom and define the seriousness of our decisions. This we must never forget. We are not dealing with the ultimate issues of the Church. Here we can deal only with immediate issues. But as far as we ourselves are concerned, we shall be dealing with ultimate issues. The motives that will control our thinking, our plans, our opinions, these are ultimate decisions. And these two things we must somehow hold together in an accent of hope. For, as Paul expresses the final certainty, "Nothing can separate us from the love of God in Christ Jesus our Lord."

In the three chapters which follow chapter 8 the argument is very intricate; but the main themes in them can be summed up in one simple phrase, "God is faithful." And God is faithful in a much wider sense than we think. We ask Paul, "Why did God accept Jacob and refuse Esau?" And he answers, "Look at what God did with Pharaoh." Pharaoh is a much darker character than Esau, but Pharaoh is part of the whole process of salvation in the Old Testament. At the Red Sea, the Israelites were delivered from Pharaoh, but so too were the Egyptians. There is both a religious event and a secular event in the same event. God's purposes are wider than we think. They include everybody. And if they include Pharaoh, why not us? If they include Judas, why not us?

So we come to the end of the argument and face the question, How do we come to our Lord? We come to him purely in terms of the certainty that he is faithful and that he will keep faith. We are saved by grace and grace alone. To use our Master's words: "Having done all, we must learn to say, I am an unprofitable servant." (Luke 17:10.) We sing, "Nothing in my hands I bring, simply to Thy cross I cling"; but there is no point in singing that if we have nothing to bring. The man who sings that has a tremendous lot to bring, but has thrown it all away and has decided to come empty-handed because none of these things really means anything. I have rendered my obedience, but I am an unprofitable servant nevertheless.

I do not know whether I have succeeded in what I attempted to do in this first chapter. It is not strictly a Bible study. All I have tried to do is to evoke a mood—the kind of mood in which alone we can listen, we can hear, we can obey—and, having done all, remember that we and our people and our churches can be kept and saved by grace alone.

CHAPTER 2

WHAT IS OUR TASK?

It has been rightly said that the era in which we live is the ecumenical era. It is a time when the churches, the world over, are finding one another, and Christians, the world over, are finding anew their place, mission, and involvement in the world. The word "ecumenical" carries both implications. It points, on the one hand, to the churches and their togetherness and, on the other hand, to the secular world, its histories, and its history. It is important that the use of the word ecumenical should carry both implications. When one denomination speaks of its world spread and its world-wide task and calls itself ecumenical, the implication of the togetherness of the churches is absent. When churches use the word ecumenical for any organization or program which is not concerned with Christian witness in and to the whole world, the other implication is absent.

For many years, the ecumenical task was conceived as the task of mission, and the missionary enterprise was the main burden of the ecumenical movement. The problems dealt with during this period were the problems of co-operation, comity, collaboration, and consultation. The problems were those set by the one mission to the several churches.

A second development was the discovery which the

churches made of one another that they were churches, with the consequent determination to seek together a common life. The problems faced in this search were primarily theological. They concerned the relation of the Tradition to the traditions. The ecumenical task became the task of making manifest the unity of the Church, and the problems were those set by the one Church to the several churches.

The next task that the churches had to face was the task of ensuring an effective Christian presence in the world. The significance of this presence to the life of the world had to be understood. The problems faced here were not only the problems of theology and co-operation but also those of strategy. The problems were those set by the one world to the several churches.

The time has come to bring all these phases of the Christian task together and to conceive of them as one task in its several dimensions.

It seems to me possible and illuminating to speak of the ecumenical task as possessing four dimensions. There is the dimension of length. The task is toward the end and until the end. There is the dimension of breadth. The task is set by the churches all around the world in their togetherness and their separation. There is the dimension of height. There is always a vertical reference to him who is Lord of all and who is constantly at work. And lastly, there is the dimension of depth. The Christian responsibility to penetrate into the life of the world in all its varied forms has to be faced.

The dimension of length is the eschatological dimension. The dimension of breadth is the ecclesiastical dimension. The dimension of height is the christological dimension. And the dimension of depth is the secular dimension.

THE DIMENSION OF LENGTH

The task in which we are engaged is not something which just goes on and on. It is going somewhere. There is a predetermined end. There is a set direction. Jesus will come again in glory. When he has accomplished that which he came to do, then he will hand the kingdom over to the Father. He taught us constantly to pray, "Our Father, thy kingdom come." Toward this end we pray and work. Our task is the task he assigned to James and John, when they asked that they be given precedence in the Father's kingdom. He said to them, "All that I can do for you is to assign your work in my kingdom. You shall drink of the cup that I shall drink of and be baptized with the baptism that I am baptized with. You, in your life and in your work, will be signs of the end." (Mark 10:35-40.) This is why Paul described the Christian community as those to whom the end has happened.

One of the difficult sayings in the Gospels is that of Jesus when he said, "The gospel must first be preached as a testimony to all the nations, then will the end come" (Matt. 24:14). This does not mean that we can decide when the end will come, but that before the end comes, pointers to it must be set up among the nations. The Church, the people of God in Jesus Christ, is the pointer. Here his rule is manifestly seen. His death is shown forth until he comes.

The discovery of the Church as *the* pointer to the end has controlled ecumenical thinking for the last twenty-five years. When the International Missionary Council held its assembly at Tambaram in 1938, it discerned the weakness of the Christian witness in which the sign above all signs was lost in a forest of signs. Dr. Stanley Jones protested at Tambaram that the Kingdom was being replaced by the Church in Christian thought. He was right to the extent that it is so easy to forget that the Church is only a pointer to the Kingdom, to God's continuing exercise of his rule. But he did not see that two decades of kingdom-centered theology had led men to a conception of Christian strategy which blurred the ultimate distinction between faith and unfaith. The Church is the company of those who believe. It is from within the Church that we discern what our obedience ought to be. The Kingdom makes that obedience possible and meaningful.

But any talk about the Church as the pointer to the Kingdom is belied when its works are not fruit but decoration. When erecting a wedding pandal we often hang coconuts on bamboos. Those coconuts are not the fruit of the bamboo. They are merely decoration. It is possible for a church to engage in activities and programs which are not the fruit of faith nor are dependent on the faithfulness of its people. Many an Ashram in India had its own financial resources and, therefore, did not become the result of the Christian obedience of the church within which it was set. At a conference in Madras, someone said that his church supported their full-time ordained ministry, except that the hierarchy was paid from abroad, and on salary scales decided abroad. In some places, a large proportion of the pastors of congregations earned their salaries as government servants. The issues involved in all these examples are complex, but in every case one of the issues is whether it is a coconut tree which is bearing coconuts or whether it is a bamboo on which coconuts have been hung.

A further implication of the eschatological dimension of the Christian task is that evangelism must be seen in relation to the task of erecting the signs of faith. Evangelism means the intention to lead men to faith in Jesus Christ. But faith itself is not something which we can communicate. He knows those who are his and he will present them blameless at the last. There is a mystery here which must constantly warn us against understanding the Church as the company of those who will ultimately populate heaven.

The eschatological reference must, on the one hand, help us to see the centrality of the Church in its rela-

tionship to the Kingdom and, on the other hand, under-
line the determining nature of the Kingdom in relation
to the Church.

THE DIMENSION OF BREADTH

There are churches in every part of the world. These
churches must share a common life, all in each place
and all throughout the world, so that the world may
recognize the one mission. The clue to the meaning
of history is that God became part of it in Jesus Christ,
and that the mission of Jesus Christ is a continuing
mission weaving together the many strands of human
history into one movement. Jesus prayed that the
Church may be one, that the world may believe in
this one mission. (John 17:21.) Were the object of
evangelism simply to win faith in Jesus Christ, the
division of the churches might not matter. But the
object of evangelism is so to win men to faith in Jesus
Christ that they will become active participants in the
central missionary movement which binds human history together. It is this participation which is hindered
by the separateness of the churches.

The dimension of breadth of the ecumenical task
lays on us the burden of manifesting the unity of the
Church. This unity is given, and as it is given, it is our
responsibility to give appropriate forms to that unity.
The World Council of Churches is a form in which a
given unity has been contained and expressed. So are

the East Asia Christian Conference and the All-Africa Conference of Churches. Even a hymnbook or a book of prayers is a form expressing a given unity. There is also the necessity to be ready with forms in which to receive unity. Forms make unity possible; unity makes forms necessary. Sometimes, to be unprepared with forms is to miss the moment and lose the gift.

One of the issues in contemporary missionary thinking is that of Joint Action for Mission. This is a question of giving form to a unity that has been affirmed through many years but which has not yet been expressed in action. At the New Delhi Assembly of the World Council of Churches, it was pointed out that there is a wide area of freedom already available for joint action. It is possible in this area for Christians of many churches to work together without prejudging theological differences and without disloyalty to conscience. It is because this area of freedom is not occupied that there is little pressure on the boundaries and, therefore, no widening of the area. Often the differences have been made an excuse for not doing anything about agreements.

The important thing is to experiment with suitable forms in which to express the unity which we have already been given. For instance, what is to prevent the congregations of two different denominations in a town from combining in a common evening service? Cannot a team ministry, such as has proved effective in the East Harlem Protestant parish, be tried in many other places and situations? In areas of new development, where new industries are growing up, where housing estates are being built, where colonization schemes are in progress, is it impossible for Christians of various denominations to come together in one worshiping congregation, using one church building and providing for common worship, with the necessary arrangements to see that everybody is able to partake of the Lord's Supper without violation of conscience?

In another aspect of the Church's life, equally far-reaching questions can be asked about the possibility of united action in Christian witness, or service, or training, or about denominational action which is part of a commonly conceived plan. The dimension of breadth is as challenging a dimension as that of length. If the dimension of length is the result of the fact that "He comes," the dimension of breadth is the result of the fact that "He gives."

THE DIMENSION OF HEIGHT

This is a result of the fact that "He works." There is always, in all Christian work and witness, the vertical reference to him who is the Master Craftsman. Our obedience depends on discerning where he is and where he is at work, and there to work with him.

At the first conference at which I heard Dr. John R. Mott speak, a conference on evangelism in India in 1937, he said that the main problem in the Church's life was that its forces were immobile. The Church, in its encounter with the world, and its service to the world, and its witness in the world, had in many places planted heavy institutions and had adopted intricate procedures of work. To put it in another way, the Church was prepared for trench warfare but found itself faced with an enemy whose methods were much more flexible. There is no use in meeting challenges which are not there, and in being silent at those places where the actual questions are being asked, where the actual problems have to be met.

It may shed some light on this issue if a collateral problem can be used as an illustration. The only theological debate which developed at the New Delhi Assembly of the World Council of Churches arose out of the statement concerning "meeting Jesus Christ in one's encounter with the unbeliever." There were those who doubted that Jesus Christ could be met and recognized in those persons and in those areas of life and thought where he was not openly confessed. They raised a question not so much about his presence but about the possibility of recognizing that presence. They also raised the question as to whether there was any obedience to him and his work within and as part of the disobedience of unfaith.

It seemed to me then, and it seems to me now, that we mistake the problem unless we see it as the problem raised by the universal presence of Jesus and the fact that that presence cannot be completely devoid of fruit anywhere. In an article written later, Dr. Niesel showed surprise that those who stood behind the Barmen Declaration should have been thought of, especially by Asians, as representing an "old view." The Barmen Declaration speaks of "Jesus Christ as the only person we must listen to." The issue in debate, however, is "Where is he?" Is he only discernible where the accents of faith are heard? The dimension of height in the Christian task must be reckoned with. It is not enough to depend solely on theological formulation to follow the Lord where he is at work. Theological formulations are necessary to set direction, but they cannot take the place of that sensitivity which only the Holy Spirit can give.

THE DIMENSION OF DEPTH

The gospel seed must be sown into the furrows of life. Every secular particularity must be penetrated by the Christian presence, and signs must there be erected to the Lord of all life. He comes, he gives, he works, he saves. His salvation is no simple salvation of the soul. It is a salvation of the whole man. It is not a salvation of persons only. It is a salvation of the whole universe. It is not just a salvation of the Christian community. It is a salvation of human history.

The Church's institutions of service and witness are an attempt to make clear the scope of this salvation in Jesus Christ, but in every new situation these institutions and their mode of operation have to be rethought. Let me attempt some examples to make clear what I mean.

There is the necessity, for instance, of demonstrating the meaning of Jesus as truth in the field of secular education. For this purpose the Church should seek to run some schools under Christian auspices; but, if the number of schools that are run cannot be sustained by the spiritual resources or the numerical strength of the Christian community to whom these schools belong, nothing is gained.

There is also the contrary truth that since a school is a normal mode of community existence, it is necessary for Christians to take their place in the community alongside their fellows. There is little justification for Christians to run schools, where it is possible for these schools to be run by all members of a community together.

There is also a third way in which this kind of problem can be approached. When a fruit tree is planted, we also plant a hedge around it to protect it from cattle. Sometimes it is as necessary to attend to the hedge as to the tree, but soon the time comes when the hedge must be removed. Christian institutions, like schools and hospitals, are largely part of the hedge. Of course, some of them are part of the tree. A school in which is demonstrated the significance of Jesus as truth is not part of the hedge. The hospital in which it is shown that Jesus brings healing to the whole man is an essential witness to the gospel. But where an institution was an obvious and necessary part of the hedge, affording protection to a new Christian community, the question must be asked constantly, Has the time come for this hedge to be torn down? That does not mean closing the school. It means only that the school should cease to be an integral part of the church structure.

There is still another way in which this problem must be viewed. Christian institutions of service often become a source of secular power for the church. Such power arouses fear or jealousy in others. It is not possible to convert either those who are afraid of us or those who are jealous of us. Indeed, the only effective way of penetrating the world with the Christian presence is to penetrate it in weakness. Those whom we would win for Christ must be able to crucify us if they want to. This is the source also of the basic questioning which must always go hand in hand with all forms of interchurch aid. The church, indeed, is one; and therefore financial resources in one part of the church can be used in another part. But can this happen without any inhibitions? The issue is never whether a church has a right to spend that money, but whether it has the spiritual resources to spend it for God's glory.

I have used the Christian institution as a negative example to make clear what it means to take the dimension of depth seriously, but no negative example will do to spell out all the many ways in which obedience to this dimension must be expressed.

The whole question of indigenization also lies in this area. The nation is a particularity which we must take seriously. This does not mean that nationality can be theologically defined or delimited. It only means that the results of secular history must be taken seriously. There is a tendency today for the churches in the West to express grave misgivings about taking the nations seriously when one is talking about the Church and its unity. World Methodism, for instance, is supposed to be a theological alternative to Methodists in a particular country uniting in one church with their fellow Christians. As I have said elsewhere, there may be some sense in Portugal's talking about Angola as part of Metropolitan Portugal. When the Church uses this kind of language, it is simply absurd.

CONCLUSION

A task in these dimensions cannot be performed without doing two things. We must learn to have that cast of mind which brings all forms of the Church's life and witness constantly under God's judgment. We must beware of the temptations to protect his gifts against himself. If God remains God, yesterday must yield to tomorrow. Sometimes this attitude of mind may push one to acts of responsible disobedience whereby settled boundaries and landmarks are challenged.

A second necessity is to recognize the urgency of the hour at which the Church stands. It is not a matter of feeling urgent but of being caught in an urgency in which God sets the pace. Here again, let me give some negative illustrations. One of the causes of the messianic movements in Africa was the utter slowness with which missionaries divested themselves of their authority and status in the life of the African churches. One of the reasons for the No-Church Movement in Japan was the unreadiness of the churches to discard their Western vesture. One of the reasons for so many sects is that the churches are so slow in finding their unity, and these sects are attempting short-cuts.

Who is sufficient for these things? The only way to answer that question is to keep looking at the task in its total dimension until one sees, not all the things that ought to be done, but the one central Figure from whom the task derives and on whom the task depends. We see him in every situation, the Prince of Life carrying his cross and going to Calvary after Calvary. The task finally for us is to walk the way with him. To some it is given, as it was given to Simon of Cyrene, to carry his cross for him. But to all of us it is given to go with him outside the city gates and there, where the securities of life and the settled landmarks of the task have been left behind, share with him his glory, both in suffering and in victory.

CHAPTER 3

HOW SHALL WE DO OUR WORK?

When we ask Christians, "What is the source of our common life?" there is always a unanimous answer, "Jesus." He is the Life. When we ask the question, "What is the source of our common faith?" the answer is "Jesus." He is the Truth. When we ask, "Have we a common task, a common work to be done in a common way?" the answer is always, "No." There is a common task but there is no common way. Methodists can do it one way; Anglicans can do it another way; Presbyterians can do it a third way. Is that true? Jesus said, "I am the life, I am the truth, I am the way." (John 14:6.)

Paul has a very revealing phrase, in his letter to the Ephesians, where he talks about "the works that God has prepared for us to walk in" (Eph. 2:10). In other words, the things we do in obedience to him are already prepared. They are prepared in the sense not only that he tells us what to do, but that he is doing them. "God at work" is one of the facts of our life that we must fully take into account. In the Acts of the Apostles, the writer says that, in the Gospel he wrote, he had already talked about "the things which Jesus began to do and to teach" (Acts 1:1). This means that, in the Acts of the Apostles, he was going to write about the things which Jesus continued to do and to teach.

47

God at work. I want to keep on stressing this. I have
already mentioned it twice in the last two chapters, but
I keep on stressing it because I think it is something we
do not fully take into account. We are here to decide
about various things. Let us simply face the fact that God
has already decided about them. And the works that we
perform are either works he has prepared for us to walk
in, or the works we have prepared. Those are our only
two alternatives. And, if we prepare our own works, we
can do these works while he continues to do the work
that he has prepared. We have somehow to take seriously
the fact that God is dependent on us and independent
of us. The Scriptures will not allow us to forget either
aspect of it.

In his high priestly prayer, Jesus prayed, "That they
may be one, that the world may believe that thou didst
send me" (John 17:21). Here the object of belief is
plainly stated. Men and women must be one in faith in
his mission and in himself as Missionary. There is only
one mission, there is only one missionary; and the object of our mission is to bring people to believe in his
mission and to participate in it. Men must see that the
history of the world is dependent on his continuing
mission, and that by that mission all history is determined and will come to its fulfillment. We often
speak of so presenting the gospel that men will accept
Jesus as their Lord and Savior. Speaking strictly, this is
not enough. More is involved in the proclamation of
the gospel than personal salvation. The gospel must be

so proclaimed that men become participants in the continuing ministry of Jesus Christ.

Here is a sentence out of Jeremiah. The Lord is speaking to his people through his prophet. "If you have raced with men on foot and they have wearied you, how will you compete with horses?" (Jer. 12:5.) The point that God is making is that "the time has come when I have got to get going." Our trouble with God is that, when we are in a hurry, he seems to go to sleep; and when he is in a hurry, we find it very difficult to catch up with him. God is simply saying, "Running with men, you got tired; but remember now you have got to run with horses." That is what we mean by saying, "A thousand ages in thy sight are like an evening gone." As the epistle explains it, God does in a moment what it takes a thousand years to do, even though for what feels like a thousand years he seems to be doing nothing. (II Pet. 3:8.) While we sweat our blood out trying to get something done, God seems to say, "Just wait," and then suddenly he is all in a hurry. This is the situation in which the Christian is caught. I believe that the hour at which we stand today is this hour of urgency, of trying to catch up with God, and of God saying to us, "You've got to run with horses."

Our task, if I may recapitulate what I have already said in a different way, is to be engaged with God in his mission. He continues in his mission. Let us never get it into our heads that Jesus has finished what he came to do and that now he has handed the business over to

us to work for him. We never work for him. We are
only allowed to work with him. He is at work all the
time. And this mission of God is to weave together into
one the history of the nations until creation has become the new creation in its wholeness.

When in Matthew's Gospel we read that Jesus told his
disciples, "Go ye into all the world and preach the
gospel, baptizing the nations and teaching them the
obedience of faith" (Matt. 28:19-20), the word "nations" means men in their several particularities of
race, of nation, of community, and of occupation. Whatever the secular particularity may be, that is what must
be brought to the obedience of faith. God loved the
world—that is, men in their several relationships. God
did not just love people.

We often say that the answer to the problems of our
world is Jesus Christ. Can I say with reverence that the
answer to the problems of our world is not Jesus Christ.
The answer to the problems of the world is the answer
that Jesus Christ provided, which is the Church. Jesus
has set in the world a community bound to him, shar-
ing his life and his mission, and endued with the power
of the Holy Spirit. This community, that is we and
others like us, is the answer that Jesus has provided for
the evils of this world. It is we who in our common
life should demonstrate the possibilities of reconcilia-
tion and peace between people, who in our common
mission should demonstrate the direction along which
history is set, who in our common hope should be able

to rescue men from despair and frustration. This is the answer which Jesus provided and which we betray when we are disloyal to him. This is why we are now thinking about how the Church can be true to its responsibility in mission, and how it may renew its structure and form so that it may fulfill in our day and generation that which is committed to it.

Let me attempt a visual method of answering the question I have raised—How shall we do our work? As I think of the world, I picture it as a circle. The center of that circle is Jesus Christ. He is Lord of all. Once in my home town of Jaffna, at a big student rally, we sang the hymn "Crown Him with Many Crowns," a very beloved hymn in Methodist circles. Dr. Visser t'Hooft was the chief speaker at that rally, and at the end of the meeting he came to me and said, "Niles, that is the first time I have heard that hymn; I don't like it at all." I said, "What is the matter with the hymn?" He said, "Jesus is already crowned. What are you people trying to do?" I think he misunderstood the meaning of the hymn, but his point was clear. We do not make Jesus Lord; he is already Lord—Lord of the world, Lord of the universe, Lord of all men, and our Lord. He does not become our Lord when we accept him as our Lord. He is my Lord whether I accept him or not. From my acknowledgment, various results follow, but he is Lord irrespective. He has been exalted, and to him a name has been given which is above every name—"that at the name of Jesus every knee shall bow"

(Phil. 2:10). The center is Jesus Christ. But in the way we do our work, we can obscure this center.

The first way is in our dealings with men of other religions. We tend to think of Christianity as a circle of which Jesus is the center; of Hinduism as another circle with its own center; of Communism as another circle with its own center, and so on. These circles lie beside one another. Evangelism is conceived as an attempt to bring a man from his circle to the Christian circle. This is what has been called the "Noah's Ark" method of evangelism—to bring the animals one by one. Surely, this is not the truth. There is only one circle of reality, and Jesus Christ is the center of it. Hinduism is simply a circle within the larger circle, even though its own center is not the real center. Jesus Christ is the center of the whole. Whether a person accepts him or not does not change the fact about Jesus. I dislike the term "non-Christian" because whenever it is used it is used adjectivally, and I do not believe it is a true adjective of any man. A person may not be a Christian, he may not have acknowledged Jesus Christ as Lord; but he cannot be a non-Christian, someone about whom there is no truth in Jesus Christ.

We obscure the center when, in speaking of men of other beliefs, we speak as if they were outside the circle whose center is Jesus Christ. Jesus is already Lord— Lord of all life and Lord of all men. He must be acknowledged Lord, but it is not this acknowledgment which makes him Lord. It is essential to remember that

Jesus Christ, in the life he lives—the life he has lived
in the flesh and the life he now lives as risen and
ascended Lord—is the common ground of true evangelism. The evangelizing activity is part of our common
work because it is part of our common life. Those whom
we would seek to win for him are already encompassed
by him.

Another way in which we obscure the center is by
pretending that our churches are circles centered on
Jesus. If we were honest we would accept the fact that
not a circle but an ellipse would best represent any one
of our churches. They have two foci: one focus is Jesus
Christ and the other focus is some specific way in which,
in the tradition of the Church, witness has been borne to
him. When we talk about church union, it is with these
traditions that we have to deal. Those who say we belong to Jesus Christ alone are simply dishonest—Paul
refers to such a group in Corinth (I Cor. 1:12). But we
also obscure the center when we are satisfied with the
ellipse. We should be seeking constantly to get the
ellipse and the circle to coincide, to bring the focus
which represents the tradition and the center closer
together. We shall never fully accomplish this, but we
should be striving for it all the time. If then there is to
be a second focus, how shall it be determined? Shall
it be determined in terms of world-wide denomina-
tionalism, or should the issue be decided in terms of a
common task in a common situation?

It is my conviction that denominations and confes-

sions throughout the world have a function to perform
of the utmost importance. They must see that their
heritage is not dissipated, that what they have severally
learned from the Lord becomes part of the heritage of
all. But the problem arises when denominations and
confessions set up world structures. To put a structure
around any particular tradition is to make it indigesti-
ble. It is much more reasonable that the second focus
be determined by the locality—the actual tasks and
actual people. Indeed, it is essential to see that the
second focus is the result of the church's involvement in
witness in the time and place where it is set. Illusions
are created where this is not recognized.

Let me give some illustrations. We are working for
church union in Ceylon. There is always the temptation
to think that we are constructing a circle, but soon
enough our Christian brethren in other parts of the
world show us that it is not a circle we have constructed
but an ellipse. The trouble is that our Christian
brethren usually go on to express their unhappiness that
the second focus in our ellipse is not the same as theirs.
The historic traditions of our mother churches in the
West must certainly guide us, but should not the form
and emphasis of our confession be determined by the
challenges with which we are faced? A confession is controlled by its essential points of negation. It is here that
the need for true indigenization arises. For, in the
countries of Asia, we shall not come to the point of
truly confessing Jesus Christ until we come to grips

with the intellectual and social challenges that are all around us. At present, most of the churches of Asia are intellectually, and in large measure even socially, isolated from their surroundings.

Let me also attempt another type of example to illustrate this importance of making the second focus relevant to the place of witness. It is an excellent principle to hold that Methodist bishops, irrespective of color, should be paid the same salary in the United States; but when this principle is applied to the Methodist Church in India, for instance, and the money to make this principle effective is provided by America, then the result is incongruous. Or again, when the East Asia Christian Conference arranges for missionaries to go from one Asian country to another, it is an excellent principle that an Asian missionary in a country should not be treated differently from a Western missionary in the same country. But to pay the Asian missionary on the same scale as the Western missionary is to create a situation which is impossible for the Asian receiving church to accept. Through all these examples, the point made is a very simple one. That the second focus should be defined within the context of a church's actual situation and the specific challenges which it faces in its mission.

We also obscure the center when we use the ellipse as our frame of reference for the mission. A bishop of the Church of South India wrote to an American mission board for assistance in a new youth program. He de-

scribed the facilities needed and the cost, and urged
the board to provide funds. A letter came back from
the board secretary asking, "What do the other churches
in the area think about this project?" Such a question
had never been asked before. But behind the asking of
this question was a true conviction that the mission of
the Church was indivisible and that the churches must
decide together not only what must be done together,
but also what must be done separately. The ellipse is
not the frame of reference for our work, the circle is.
It is true that we cannot do more than draw an ellipse,
but we must never forget that constantly we have to be
breaking away from the ellipse and breaking the ellipse
in order to render our obedience. The whole idea of
Joint Action for Mission is in this effort to move away
from the ellipse toward the circle. Mission board secretaries have often asked me, "If we apply the procedures
and principles involved in Joint Action for Mission,
will there not be resentment in Asia?" But who gave
Americans or British the responsibility to make Asians
happy!

Let me illustrate this last point. When the mission
board secretary related to the Jaffna Diocese of the
Church of South India came to Ceylon recently, he
called for consultation representatives of the C.S.I., together with representatives of the Anglican and Methodist churches. This was the first time in Ceylon that
the secretary of a mission board had asked for consultation with members of churches other than the one his

mission board was related to. At this consultation he explained that it was impossible for a mission agency responsibly to participate in the work of mission in a country unless the mission took precedence over the interest and needs of one particular church. As another secretary of a mission board said at another consultation, a mission agency must be prepared to support the cause of mission without expecting a denominational dividend. In terms of the old bilateral relationship, the church concerned asked for help from its related mission agency in terms of its own program. But there was no attempt to have this program assessed in terms of a common strategy of mission worked out by all the churches. Surely the need is to devise immediately the procedures which are necessary to ensure that, in the use of funds and the deployment of missionary personnel, both the sending and the receiving churches have an equal right of decision, and also that in the decisions which are made it is the mission which is determinative.

Finally, we obscure the center by the way in which we assess priorities as far as the use of time and money is concerned. The National Christian Council in a country, for instance, is an attempt to serve the circle, at least to serve more than one ellipse; but again and again the leaders of the churches are so busy serving their own ellipses that they have no time to go beyond them. The bishop simply says, "I have no time," and sends some young clergyman to represent his church at the N.C.C., so does the moderator; and soon everybody is complaining that the N.C.C. is neither serving the circle nor the ellipse. The same attitude is apparent in the way in which many church leaders respond to invitations to consultations convened by such bodies as the World Council of Churches or the East Asia Christian Conference. I would grant that the problem of time is a real one, but before this problem can be solved there must be a thorough commitment to priorities. There is no other way in which we can be constantly challenging the ellipse except by taking every opportunity to go beyond it.

There is another example that can be used here. We often assess the maturity of a church by its ability to wear the armor that has become traditional. The present administrative and financial structures of most of the churches in Asia are reproductions of similar structures in the West and have little relationship to the financial and social realities of our own countries. The issue of self-support is wrongly stated if the form of the structure to be supported is not changed. The churches of Asia have to find a basic financial structure which is not dependent on aid from outside and which is possible because it is related to the actualities of its own financial setting. The point is that since an ellipse is all that is possible, the second focus must be set within an actual situation.

Paul, writing to the Corinthians, urges on them the fact that he begat them in Christ. (I Cor. 4:15.) We in

Asia, too, came to find Christ through the ministry of some particular denomination. But when the church's debt to Paul became a matter of controversy, and parties in the church of Corinth began to make his name a party name, he exclaimed: "Is Christ divided?" (I Cor. 1:13), or as Moffatt translates, "Has Christ been parceled out?" Let us accept the fact that it is only an ellipse which we can draw, but let us never forget the fact that since it is an ellipse it has to be our ellipse and not somebody else's.

Let me conclude by pointing to three truths which can be, for us, resources for our obedience. The first truth is a negative one. If I do not want to paint, of what use would it be if God should grant me the vision of the painter? One might say I could appreciate what somebody else paints, but in the Christian life the spectator is an irrelevance. Christian obedience means participation. Is it not possible that the call to Joint Action for Mission among us who belong to several churches remains a puzzle, not because the plan is not clear, but because some wrong personal attitudes have robbed us of vision. In the last analysis it is a resource for obedience that the place of my responsibility is the place of my soul. It is here that the call to repentance comes.

Secondly, it is a resource for obedience that I do not have final responsibility for deciding what is right and wrong in any ultimate sense. In the controversy in which he was involved in the Corinthian church, Paul makes three statements. He says to the people of Corinth, "I am not right because I think I am right. Nor am I right because some of you think I am right. Nor am I wrong because some of you think I am wrong." (I Cor. 4:3-4.) In all the differences of opinion in which we shall find ourselves, it is in this spirit that we shall need constantly to engage in the search for what is right. Besides, the release which comes from this knowledge of our situation is enhanced by the fact that we know that the God we serve can also be fully trusted with our mistakes.

And finally, there is the resource of God's grace. Smoking flax he does not quench. A bruised reed he does not break. (Matt. 12:20.) How often have we found it true that when our light had grown dim and the wick was simply smoking, he did not throw away the wick but set it alight again, retwisting the wick and pouring oil into the little lamp. When, because the reed was cracked, the music was not clear and the tone was gone, he did not throw away the reed as well he might, but repaired it until it produced music again. The riverbank was full of reeds. He could have thrown away that reed and got himself another one. The wick was just a piece of cloth. He could have thrown it away and got another piece. I was expendable but he did not dismiss me from his service. So were you. There lies our hope and our confidence. There lies also the ground of our final responsibility.

CHAPTER 4

WHERE DO OUR TEMPTATIONS LIE?

We have been speaking about the nature and certainties of our faith, the nature and responsibilities of our task, and the ways in which both the task and the faith demand that we should work. In this chapter we shall look at the question, Where do our temptations lie?

There are many ways in which such a subject can be treated; but again, purely to avoid the risk of dealing with those questions that I would like to include in my own way, I have chosen to deal with some of the main issues that Israel and the Church faced as we read about them in the Scriptures. These were the classic temptations, if I may call them that. We can identify in the Bible a number of situations in which the Church, through the centuries, was tempted to compromise its faith, and see how the prophets and pastors and leaders of the Church saved it from such compromise. I have chosen to deal with nine such situations.

The first three belong to the period from Moses to Elijah, during which period the central issue in debate was—Who is the God we worship and how must we worship him? The second three belong to the period from King Hezekiah to John the Baptist. This period was characterized by a succession of reform movements within Israel. Here the issue was—What does it mean to be God's people? The last three belong to the period of the New Testament church. In different forms, they deal with the question of the relation between the Church and the world. Let us then deal with these nine temptations in order.

1. The first temptation was that faced by the people of Israel when Moses went up Mount Sinai and took so long to return. One day the people got so restless that they came to Aaron and said, "We do not know when Moses will come back, and it is a long time since we had a religious festival. We want to have one now. Give us a god whom we can worship." So Aaron made for them a golden calf and gave it to them, and they said, "These are your gods, O Israel, who brought you up out of the land of Egypt" (Exod. 32:4). It is significant that when the kingdom was divided into two, this act was repeated again by King Jeroboam, who built the temple at Bethel and installed there two golden calves. (I Kings 12:28.)

But why the golden calf? Because that was a symbol they knew all about. It is essential to remember that they did not say, "We shall worship the golden calf instead of Yahweh." What they said was, "This is Yahweh. We shall worship Yahweh through the golden calf." Aaron did not ask them to give up one god and acknowledge another one. What he was doing was to give them the worship of Yahweh in the form they understood best, the form of fertility. Fertility is a primary motive of religion as religion, whether that religion be old or new.

Some of us who came to Evanston, in the United States of America, in 1954, for the Assembly of the World Council of Churches, were intrigued by the various billboards and displays in Evanston at that time. I want to refer here to a notice that was found in most of the streetcars and buses. It was in two parts. On one side it said, "Come and see our seed plots"; on the other side it said, "Prayer works." Underneath was the explanation. A group of people had divided their piece of land into two. Having sown on both sides, they had prayed over one side and not over the other. They claimed that the side which they had prayed over was giving a better yield. Here was proof that prayer works. This was exactly what Aaron was talking about—fertility, Yahweh under the sign of the golden calf.

To give another illustration from an incident that happened at Evanston, I would like to refer to President Eisenhower's address before the delegates to the assembly. The subject of his address was "The Logistics of Faith." The main thing that he told us was that, in the kind of world in which we were living, the only thing that would help us was faith. It did not matter what kind. It did not have to be faith in Jesus Christ. In other words, let us have religion, for that alone can help men to meet the challenges of life. One of my friends used to remark, commenting on this attitude, "It is no good saying, faith is all you want, it does not matter what kind. This is like saying you are all right as long as you have francs. But it makes a world of difference whether they are French francs or Swiss francs. It is not enough to have dollars. It makes a big difference whether they are Malayan dollars or U.S. dollars."

Let me give another illustration, again from the United States. I read in the newspapers about a pilgrimage to Washington organized by American churchmen in 1951. This pilgrimage was received by President Truman, and, in receiving it, he said he wished that the churches could be organized together in order that they might be mobilized to bring peace to the world. Bishop Angus Dun replied to the President in these words: "The God who makes himself known to us in the Scriptures, who makes himself known to us in Christ, cannot be bargained with, cannot be mobilized or used for human purposes however good. He can only be trusted and loved and served. There are frightened servants of mammon who think that this might be a good time to mobilize the Church to fight Communism and its godlessness, so that mammon might be served in peace."

The issue here is exactly the same as that faced by the people of Israel when Aaron gave them the golden calf. The story of the golden calf is not about some far-away event. It is about us and about a temptation that lies within our own hearts.

Let me give one more illustration. A lady who was a member of my church came to me one day with a problem. She had had no children after her marriage, and the doctors were unable to help her. She undertook a vow to the Virgin Mary at a Roman Catholic shrine, but still she had no child. Then she went and made a vow at a Hindu shrine in one of the Hindu places of pilgrimage. After this, she had a child. Her question to me was, "Don't you think I must become a Hindu?" I told her that, in terms of what she wanted, it did not make any difference to what religion she belonged. If fertility or prosperity is to be the determining consideration, then the Christian faith is already compromised.

Among the religions today, there are four major movements which represent the position that the form through which God is worshiped does not matter, and therefore advocate syncretism. There is the teaching that stems from Ramakrishna which puts the various religions together on the basis of Hinduism; theosophy puts them together on the basis of Buddhism; Bahaiism puts them together on the basis of Islam; and the M.R.A. puts them together on the basis of Christianity. In all these four, the one question which is never raised is about the identity of God.

This particular temptation can present itself also in another way. Let me again give an illustration. I was talking one day to a group of theological students in one of the seminaries in America, at what they call a bull session. We talked for about half an hour, but they did not understand what I was saying nor did I understand what they were saying. Then one of the students said to

me, "Sir, we shall try again. I will put it in a very simple
way and you will understand what we are trying to say.
As far as we are concerned, the Resurrection and the
Incarnation are the same event." I put my head within
my hands and said, "As far as I am concerned, there are
thirty years in between." "But you are talking about the
Gospels," they said. "We are talking about the Christian
experience. When I find Christ, that is the Incarnation,
that is also the Resurrection."

Here is the danger of divorcing the Christian experience from the gospel event, so that the ground of faith is
not in the Christ story but in me and what I feel able
to experience or believe. Gandhiji said, in one of his last
prayer meetings, "I believe in the resurrection of Christ:
by that I mean, I believe that the sacrifice of the cross
is the ultimate reality." From where the religious experience or the religious conviction as such is the basis
of faith, it is a small step to the practices of Subud or
Zen, which are intended to produce religious experience
apart from the particularities that belong to any religion. The particular in the faith of Israel was provided by an act of God. What was central was not the
experience of deliverance from Egypt but that it was
God who delivered them and that therefore they belonged to God. Their deliverance by itself could be
celebrated through the worship of the golden calf, but
between the God who delivered them and all that the
calf symbolized, there could be no compromise.

2. The second temptation arose when the people of

Israel came to settle down in Canaan. These people, who were nomads, shepherds, and fighters, when they came to Canaan settled down to an agricultural way of life. The Canaanites among whom they lived taught them to plow, to sow, and to reap. They also instructed them in the various religious practices that went with this plowing, sowing, and reaping. They said to the Israelites, "Your god is a god of war; our gods are gods of agriculture. There is no need for you to give up your god. But if you want really to succeed as an agricultural people, you must take over our gods as well." (See Judg. 2:12, 13; I Sam. 12:10.)

"Yahweh—through" was the temptation in the wilderness; "Yahweh—and" was their temptation in Canaan. This desire to put one's trust in other things, along with one's trust in God, is a very natural desire. God, because he is God, cannot be manipulated or exploited. He remains outside man's control. Therefore, there is the temptation also to relate life and its needs to a form of religion in which success can be ensured by correct practice. Such forms of religion abound. They belong to the ancient history of man as he sought to come to terms with the world in which he had to live. They are an amalgam of wishful thinking, magic, and superstition, and of correlated human experience. They represent the dictates of prudence in the conduct of life.

My part of the world is full of illustrations of this particular attitude and temper. Somebody comes to me and says, "Sir, my daughter is getting married, and I want the service to take place on Saturday morning at nine o'clock." I look at my schedule and say, "I am sorry, but on Saturday morning at nine o'clock we are having the church meeting, and this cannot be postponed. Why not have the marriage on Saturday afternoon or on Friday?" But he is very reluctant to do this. He keeps insisting that it should be on Saturday morning at nine o'clock. And ultimately, when one gets down to it, one discovers that he has gone to an astrologer who has told him that Saturday morning at nine o'clock is the auspicious time. The marriage must take place in church, but that by itself is not enough. It has to be "Jesus Christ—and."

The issue which has to be faced is whether one is willing to receive at God's hands that which God gives, or whether one has to add to the worship of God because of the desire somehow to get what one wants. The very first temptation which Scripture speaks about is concerning who is to decide between good and evil. God said, "I must decide. You must not." Man said, "I want to decide what is good for me." (Gen. 3:5.) The psalmist exclaims, "In thy right hand are joys for evermore." (Ps. 16:11.) The psalmist knew that whatever God gave he could rejoice in those gifts. The prophet Habbakuk took the issue further when he said that he would rejoice in God even if God gave nothing. (Hab. 3:17-18.) For a life with empty spaces means that the emptiness is filled by God's presence. Habbakuk knew the difference between receiving God's gifts and receiving God. To insist on worshiping God, because of the gifts he brings or because of the gifts we want him to bring, is not to worship God but to worship Santa Claus.

There is another way in which I would like to state this issue. When Jesus met Levi in the customs house, He said to him, "Leave your books and come and follow me" (Matt. 9:9). When the rich man came to Jesus, he said to him, "Give away all you have and come and follow me" (Mark 10:21). Jesus gave no reasons; he attempted no persuasion; there was no question of pros and cons. But when the devil came to Jesus, he was able in every case to point out the advantages of Jesus' doing as he suggested. He took him to a high mountain and showed him the kingdoms of the world. (Matt. 4:3-10.) The devil always shows us the distant scene; he hides only the precipice at the end of the road. God, on the other hand, makes only the next step plain. We must trust him for the rest, but such trust is what we find difficult. It means *God alone,* and so we make the situation more bearable by saying, *God also.*

This is not to say that there is no room for prudence in the Christian way of life. There is. But when one has heard a definite word or received a particular challenge from God, then prudence becomes unbelief.

At this point there are many things about which we argue, and about which we shall differ, and about which we must make up our minds. But there will also be those two or three things about which we know what God wants us to do. At those points, we need the grace

to look beyond the risks and to say "No" to the prompt-
ings of prudence. He who commands also promises, "I
shall be with you all the way" (Matt. 28:20) .

I cannot resist adding here a thought which has suggested itself to me through a particular passage of Scripture. In the story of Elijah and the widow of Zarephath
there is one circumstance in the story which is very significant. There was every reason for her to refuse to
look after Elijah. He was an Israelite, she was a Sidonian.
He worshiped Yahweh, she worshiped her own gods. He
was a man, she was a woman. And what was more, she
was a very poor widow. But she gave none of these
reasons to excuse herself from what Elijah asked her
to do, though any one of these reasons by itself, and
certainly all of them together, would have been a sufficient excuse. (I Kings 17:8-16.) Is it not true that often
it is when we have good reasons for not doing some act
of service or witness that we must not give these reasons?
For there will always be good reasons to say "No" to
the demand which has come when the demand is to
walk the second mile, or to forgive the twentieth time,
or to break the jar of ointment, or to leave father and
mother, or to give away all that one possesses, and so on
and so on. It is the very unpredictability of God which
makes it so desirable to be able to include in one's life
additional safeguards.

In dealing with this particular temptation that Israel
faced in Canaan, we must note also a specific form in
which Israel effected a compromise. The people brought

into the temple of Yahweh itself the "Asherim." (II Kings 13:6.) The worship of Yahweh was made to include the worship of the Asherim. Again and again, as I reflect on all the things that occupy my time as a minister in the church, I ask myself the question—How much of my work is concerned with assisting my people in the worship of the Asherim, and how much of it consists in assisting them in the worship of God? For instance, it is right that there should be prayer on special occasions—when the foundation for a new house is laid, when people move into a new house, when a new business is being opened, when a birthday is being celebrated, when a marriage or funeral anniversary is being observed, and so on: but in all these a true remembrance of God and gratitude to him are often inextricably mixed with the idea of doing something which is thought to be necessary in order to be blessed in the normal business of living. The eye is fixed rather on the blessing to be received than on God who gives it.

Similarly, there can be and often is a mixture of intention in the public worship of God. For instance, there is a difference between offering beauty to God in his worship and worshiping beauty in the guise of worshiping God. Or there is a difference between allowing religion to shape the culture of a people and making religion simply part of a cultural heritage. Or there is the difference between religious practice which is made habitual and of engaging in religious practice because, in the society to which one belongs, that is the expected thing to do. It is by ignoring these kinds of differences that faith in Jesus Christ itself is compromised, and his worship becomes simply the context in which it is not he who is worshiped but the Asherim.

3. The third great temptation which Israel faced occurred during the time of King Ahab. (I Kings 16: 31-33.) Ahab married a princess of Tyre. When she came to Jerusalem, she brought with her the worship of the Phoenician god Melkaart. She built for Melkaart a temple in Jerusalem. All she asked for was coexistence. Let the people of Israel worship their God, and let the people of Tyre worship theirs. Indeed, anybody can worship the god they choose, the god they like. But Elijah, the prophet, would have none of it. He claimed that one god was true and that the other was false, that the one was God and the other was simply vanity. "The *Elohim* were *elilim*." (Jer. 2:11.) Coexistence may be good policy, but it compromises the nature of truth.

When I assumed duties as secretary of the Department of Evangelism in the World Council of Churches, I discovered one thing as I went through the earlier correspondence in the files and as I began my own correspondence. I discovered that, speaking generally, almost everybody in the churches was quite sure that it was important to evangelize but very few seemed to be anxious that people were not getting evangelized. One of my friends once told me that he had organized an evangelistic campaign in a remote village in Ceylon, where there was no church and which was not near any church. He said, "We made careful arrangements about transport, about musicians to take part in the campaign, about literature to be distributed and about food and lodging for the evangelistic team. We even took a doctor with us." But he remarked, "If anybody had got converted and asked to become a Christian, we would not have known what to do. We made no plans about that."

Evangelism has become, in many minds, something which a church must do, but not something that must happen to people. A few stray conversions we would hope for, but fundamentally we believe in and are satisfied with coexistence. Let each have his own religion. Let each worship God in the way he likes. Am I caricaturing ourselves who are Christians? Perhaps, to some extent, I am. But it is so rare to meet someone who is really troubled because his neighbor, or her companion, does not know Jesus Christ.

There is also a second factor to be reckoned with when we are talking about the compromise which is involved in the attitude of coexistence. For coexistence is not only sought as the true relation between religions but also as the true relation between religious communities. In the Turkish empire, the Christian community was a separate political entity. It lived in scattered groups, and these "millets," as the groups were called, had separate recognition in law. But the law which afforded them this recognition also constituted for them a boundary which they could not cross.

This solution in terms of coexistence was true not

only of the Turkish empire, but it is also the accepted situation in all Muslim lands. John Taylor, the General Secretary of the Church Missionary Society, puts the matter in this way: "The traditional Muslim treatment of the Christian minority has always been to wall it in. More tolerant, up to a point, than Christendom has been in the past toward Muslims, Islam grants the church freedom to exist but it must remain a communal affair, restricted to its own ghetto. The walls are rising around the newer 'missionary' churches in the Muslim lands, just as they rose long ago around the 'ancient' churches. One Anglican compound I visited in Haifa remains in my memory as a symbol. The church, the pastor's house, and the group of institutional buildings were ringed with a high wall topped by a barbed wire fence, and the fence sloped inward, as if its purpose were not so much to exclude intruders as to keep the inmates in. Somehow, in Iran, in the Arab world, and in Israel, the Church must leap over the wall or perish."

It is certainly true that one reason for this separated political and social existence of the Christian community is that, in its family structure, it cannot live according to the common law in many lands. Even in India there is a separate Indian Christian Marriage act. In some lands Christians also need to have a different law of inheritance. But the final result of this separateness is that the Christian community tends to accept it as its normal situation.

At the Assembly of the East Asia Christian Conference

held at Bangkok, Bishop Chandu Ray of Pakistan said that, in his opinion, it would be a good thing if for a few years the church refused to baptize people. Everybody sort of looked up in dismay and wondered how it was that an Anglican bishop was talking about stopping baptism. The bishop explained himself by saying, "In Pakistan, and I believe also in India, baptism has come to mean entrance into a communal group. It is a wall that separates us as Christians from our fellow citizens." The point which the bishop was making must be well taken. Instead of being a sign of community, baptism has become, in so many places, a sign of communality. Instead of the Church being identifiable because it is the Church of Jesus Christ, the Christian community has become identifiable because it has identifiable social frontiers.

The fact of the matter is that, while coexistence renders the Christian community socially irrelevant and religiously ineffective, it also confers on it a certain kind of security. There is something to be said for a minority, and particularly a scattered minority, having not only churches to worship in, but also having their own schools in which to educate their children, their own hospitals to which they go when they are ill, their own orphanages and old-age homes to meet such special need, and their own control of employment opportunities to find employment for their youth. But precisely at this point is the temptation. Social security can and does become a preoccupation of a minority, but the temptation has to be faced. In his book *The Dome and the Rock,* Dr. Kenneth Cragg has a chapter entitled "The Art of Being a Minority." John Taylor, quoting from this chapter, puts together into one paragraph the following sentences taken from it:

In the last resort minorities have to exist with their ultimate securities outside their own direct power and control. . . . Minorities need to recognise that some of their precariousness in fact arises from the means they took, or take, to protect themselves. . . . In all situations of admitted insecurity, men are all too prone to find danger where it is not present. Are we to be so preoccupied with communal survival, with defences against hypothetical eventualities damaging to us, that we do not see and seize occasions of large-hearted ministry in a changing world?

The issue which Elijah posed was not whether there was one god or many gods. The issue about monotheism was a later issue in Jewish religious history. The question he raised was whether the people of Israel could accommodate into *their* faith and conviction the worship of other gods alongside the worship of Yahweh. It is no answer to the question which Elijah raised to say that there is only one God and that we are monotheists. The question is whether our faith in the one God is compulsive enough to make us claim all things and all men for him. Where this compulsion is absent, coexistence becomes an acceptable compromise.

4. The second group of three temptations revolves

about the question, What does it mean to be God's people? From King Hezekiah to John the Baptist, we trace, in the story of Israel, a succession of reform movements which sought to render Israel worthy of its calling. The first reform movement was initiated by King Hezekiah. The chief thing he did was to destroy the brazen serpent which was in the temple. This brazen serpent was the one which Moses had made in the wilderness and which was raised by him to be the symbol of God's forgiving mercy when the children of Israel were bitten by serpents as God's judgment upon them. Ever since, the brazen serpent had remained, for the people of Israel, the symbol of God's grace. But Hezekiah saw that it had become a false symbol because it suggested to the people that God's grace was not only free but also cheap. Since forgiveness has to be free, because no one can earn it, it must necessarily lead to the resolve to live worthily of such free forgiveness. If, on the other hand, forgiveness is taken for granted and does not issue in amendment of life, then the whole position has been compromised. Hezekiah saw clearly what the consequences of such a compromise would be. (II Kings 18:2-6.)

The Christian knows that his forgiveness was wrought by an act of God in Jesus Christ. He knows also that this forgiveness is never an act once for all, but is, in its essence, an act by which the sinner is incorporated into the continuing life of Jesus Christ. This means that the forgiven sinner is incorporated in the life of the Crucified and therefore involved in the fellowship of his sufferings. It means that the forgiven sinner finds his own forgiveness only as he shares in the total forgiving activity of God. Jesus said, "If you do not forgive others their trespasses against you, neither will you be forgiven your trespasses against God." (Matt. 6:14-15.) This is not a bargain which God makes. The point simply is that here we have not two transactions but one. Forgiveness is an indivisible whole. It is God's forgiveness of all men and, therefore, includes their forgiveness of one another.

Jesus gave us a parable to illustrate this truth. There was a man who borrowed some money from his master, promising to repay it within a certain time. When the time was up, the master called him and asked for the money. "You promised," he said, "to give me this month the hundred rupees which you borrowed. Where is the money?" The man replied, "Sir, I thought I could, but now I cannot. My wife fell ill unexpectedly and I have had more expense this last year than I anticipated. Please forgive me." The master forgave him. Then the servant went out and met a fellow servant to whom he had lent ten rupees. He said to him, "Where are the ten rupees I lent you last month? You promised to repay them today." The man said, "Please forgive me. I thought I could give the money back to you today, but I put that ten rupees on a horse in the races and it came fourth." But the servant said, "You must repay it. I cannot forgive you." When this incident was reported to the master, he called the first servant and said to him,

"What is this that I hear? When I forgave you your hundred rupees, were not the ten rupees you loaned also forgiven? For those ten rupees were part of the hundred rupees which I gave you. But now that you are not prepared to ratify my forgiveness of that ten rupees, neither can you enjoy my forgiveness of the total money I lent you." The point of the story is very clear. Forgiveness is an indivisible transaction. (Matt. 18:23-35.)

The very first temptation of the New Testament church was the temptation to avoid the cross. When Simon Peter said to Jesus, "Thou art the Christ," the Christian confession was being made for the first time. But immediately thereafter he remonstrated with his Master, because Jesus said that the Christ must suffer. (Matt. 16:22.) The cross of Christ does not represent a substitute for the cross which we must carry. The brazen serpent does not represent a God who makes no demand. It is an insidious temptation when those who live by God's grace begin to take that grace for granted. When they do so, they are simply nursing a false security.

5. The second reform movement in Israel took place under King Josiah. Up to that time, the various sacrifices were offered in many temples scattered all over the land. This led not only to laxity in ritual but also meant that there was no central religious discipline in the community. Josiah ordered that, in future, the sacrifices could be made only in the temple of Jerusalem. So Jerusalem became, for the people, the center of their re-

ligious and national life. It gave them a sense of unity as
a people, and a sense of identity as the people of God.
(II Kings 22 ff.)

But soon this very achievement became a source of
great temptation. When Jerusalem was threatened by
Babylon, the people said, "Nothing can happen to us,
for Jerusalem is the city of God and in it is God's
temple." The prophet Jeremiah had to warn them that
theirs was a false security. They thought that they were
safe because they felt that God would not allow them
to be destroyed, as such destruction would mean the
destruction of God's temple itself. They had identified
God's cause with their causes. They had come to think
of themselves as somehow indispensable to God. (Jer.
7:4.)

This temptation to involve God in the human situation is what the ancient story of the tower of Babel is
about. They said, "Let us build a tower that reaches up
to heaven to God's dwelling place." (Gen. 11:1-9.) But
God would not allow it. God never does. Dr. Walter
Freytag used to say, "We live out of God against God."
That is, we take the gifts that God has given to us, the
causes he has committed into our hands, and make them
idols over against him.

The reform under Josiah had also another result. Out
of it came the teachings that are now gathered together
in the book of Deuteronomy. Out of it arose also the
temper of mind which the book of Deuteronomy reflects.
God blesses the righteous and punishes the unrighteous.

Prosperity is a sign of blessing; adversity is a sign of judgment. Here was a reversal of the position which we saw prevailed during the reign of King Hezekiah and with which Hezekiah had to contend. Hezekiah's concern was lest people make for themselves a false security because they thought that grace was cheap. The Deuteronomists were teaching the people a false security by pretending that righteousness was humanly possible. Indeed, this pretence was plausible only because righteousness was looked upon as observance of the community discipline which the reform movement set forward. Here again Jeremiah had to tell them that what was necessary was not another version of the law, a "deutero-nomos," but renewal of the covenant.

Behold, the days are coming, says the Lord, when I will make a new covenant with the house of Israel and the house of Judah. . . . I will put my law within them, and I will write it upon their hearts; and I will be their God, and they shall be my people. And no longer shall each man teach his neighbour and each his brother, saying, know the Lord, for they shall all know me, from the least of them to the greatest, for I will forgive their iniquity and I will remember their sin no more. (Jer. 31:31-34.)

The only basis of security is God's forgiveness as it issues in a permanent relationship with him which he himself maintains.

6. The third reform movement is the one that was initiated by Ezra and Nehemiah. It was a movement

which was concerned with the purity of the race as well as the codification of the tradition. Its motto is well expressed in the words which were used by the Jews in their controversy with Jesus. "We are the children of Abraham." (Matt. 3:9; John 8:39.) Here was a security that was based on the very calling of God itself. God had called Abraham and had covenanted with him. God had maintained this covenant throughout the years with the descendants of Abraham. He had been with them in their faithfulness and faithlessness. He had forgiven them and punished them. He had sent them into exile and brought them back. Their very history was proof that God was with them and that God would remain with them.

It must have been with a sense of shock, therefore, that they heard John the Baptist say, "Do not presume to say to yourselves, we have Abraham as our father; for I tell you, God is able from these stones to raise up children to Abraham" (Matt. 3:9).

God's covenant with Abraham was that in him the nations of the world would be blessed. So that the story of the children of Abraham, with all its ups and downs, was a pointer to the fact that God's intention to bless the nations was a permanent one. It was a misreading of their history for Israel to think that God's patience and faithfulness toward them was the guarantee that, in spite of everything, they would always be secure. John the Baptist had to tell them that God could and would set them aside, if they did not serve his purposes. "Even now," said John, "the axe is laid to the root of the tree; every tree therefore that does not bear good fruit is cut down and thrown into the fire." (Matt. 3:10.)

This temptation to make its divine calling the basis of its security is one which the Church, and the churches, have constantly to resist. God's concern for the world and the peoples of the world is an overriding concern. Every Christian congregation and every church must serve that concern or be prepared to be set aside. The warning given to the church in Ephesus is apposite to every church, "If not, I will come to you and remove your lampstand from its place" (Rev. 2:5).

7. We now pass to a consideration of the third group of temptations. Here, as we have said before, the point at issue was the relation between the church and the world. In the first group of temptations, the question was how to maintain faith in God who was the God of their redemption amidst alien beliefs and practices. In the second group of temptations, the question was wherein their security lay as the people of God. In the third group of temptations, the question was how to relate themselves to the pressures and problems of the world.

The first controversy which the Church faced, as it spread in the Roman world, was the controversy over the conditions which Gentiles must fulfill when they become Christians. A party of Jewish Christians held that the Gentiles must also be circumcised and adopt

the Jewish way of life. It was this position that was
opposed strenuously by Paul. (Acts 15:1.)

"That they become like us" is the constant temptation to which the Church is exposed as it seeks to prose-
cute its mission. I remember how, at a conference on
evangelism which I attended as a youth, I heard a report
read on the work of evangelism that was being done
among Hindus in a particular area. The report said
that there was hope that one particular family would
soon be baptized and become Christians because already
they had begun to eat beef. I took a Hindu friend of
mine to attend a Christian wedding. It was the first time
he had come to church to attend a Christian wedding.
After the marriage service was over, he asked me why
the bride wore a long veil, and what the significance
of all the flower girls and page boys was. I asked him
what he had in mind in putting this question. His answer was that the people who were married were Tamils
but that none of these things was part of Tamil culture.
"I am just curious to know," he said, "whether they
have any Christian religious significance." I had to ex-
plain to him that we Christians did these things because this was how we were taught to do them by the
Western missionaries.

The desire that they become like us and the willingness that we become like them is the temptation which,
in the early church, was called Judaizing. Of course,
the unity of the whole community is easier to foster
when there is also uniformity, not only in religious

convictions and practice but also in cultural style. But it is precisely this kind of unity which the early church set aside as undesirable. It is legitimate that each cultural group bring its own culture into the household of faith.

The demand to Judaize is still present in the churches, and is made both on cultural and denominational grounds. It arises because of the assumption that the way we do it is the right way. When somebody does not do it our way, we feel as surprised as though a child had said, "I don't like jam."

8. In the early church there was not only this drive toward achieving the unity of the religious community, there was also the attempt to make the necessary accommodation to achieve social unity between Christians and those who were not. The Council of Jerusalem had asked Gentile Christians not to eat meat sacrificed to idols. (Acts 15:20.) Later the issue arose as to whether, when one bought meat in the market or when one ate as a guest in a pagan home, the Christian should question whether the meat had been sacrificed to idols; and Paul gave the advice that it was unnecessary to raise the question because idols did not represent any reality at all. He said that the only thing to take care of was that by the exercise of such freedom, no one was misled. (I Cor. 8:4 ff.)

This teaching of Paul, still later on was made the basis of what is called, in the book of Revelation, the Nicolaitan principle. (Rev. 2:14, 15.) The problem was that, by then, there were many artisans who were Christians, who were therefore naturally involved in the activities of their respective trade guilds. When these guilds met for their periodic banquets, the meat served was meat offered to the patron god or goddess of the guild. The teaching of the Nicolaitans was that such meat could be eaten. The author of the book of Revelation contested this teaching. He said that this was compromise for the sake of economic security.

It is always a moot question as to how far we can accommodate the demands which are made on us by society, when the demands are enforced by the law of the land, and how far such accommodation is legitimate when one has still the freedom to choose. For instance, there is a growing tendency in Ceylon to hold various types of public meetings and social functions on a Sunday. My own practice is never to accept an invitation for any such function. But the situation will radically change, should Sunday become an ordinary working day in Ceylon. The question always is how a Christian should exercise his freedom, when he is free; and, when he is not free, the conditions under which a Christian must refuse to obey the law of the state even though it is the law. In any case, the temptation to compromise in order to achieve economic security is a real one.

9. The third temptation which the Church faced was the temptation related to the need for achieving political unity. The Roman Empire put an end to the state of perpetual war between various tribes that was part of the life of that ancient world. Under the Caesars, politi-

cal unity was achieved. The question arose as to finding a symbol for this political unity; and the decision was taken to set up, throughout the empire, statues of the emperor before which the citizens would annually burn incense. The intention was not to institute Caesar worship as a substitute for other religions, but to ask that everybody of whatever faith should acknowledge the supremacy of Caesar. To the Christians, at that time, this was unthinkable compromise because they believed that Jesus was Lord, not only of eternity but also of time, that he exercised kingship not only over the life to come but also over this life, that he controlled not only the history of individual men and women but that he also was sovereign over nations and peoples. A political unity built around a confession that this world and its history belonged to Caesar was quite impossible. (Rev. 2:13.)

The Judaizing problem was a problem of ensuring cultural homogeneity. The problem of the Nicolaitans was how to get economic security. The problem of Caesar worship was how to achieve political unity. The problems themselves are valid. But there is no true solution for them, should that solution seek to compromise the universality of the gospel, or the absolute sovereignty of the Lord, or the locality and particularity of the Christian people—"of all in each place."

Let me close with a reference to our Lord's own temptations. It is said of him that, after his baptism, "He was led by the Holy Spirit into the wilderness to be tempted by the devil." (Matt. 4:1.) It seems a strange thing to say, but the right place to meet the devil is to meet him on the path of obedience. Should we be on the path of disobedience, the devil need not bother with us. He can leave us to our own devices.

CHAPTER 5
WHEN IS THE
CHURCH
THE CHURCH?

Sadhu Sundar Singh was traveling in a train one day.
His companion, a Hindu, thought he was a Hindu
Sadhu. As they talked, Sundar Singh produced a copy
of the New Testament and said, "I am a Christian; this
is my book." When the other man discovered that he
was a Christian, he became quite angry. He grabbed
the New Testament, tore it, and threw it out of the
train window. Someone walking along the railway
track picked up a few pages and took them home to
read. They spoke to his need. He then set out to search
for the people to whom the book belonged. There are
two entities which are inextricably bound together—
a people and a book. The Bible does not stand alone.
It is a book about the saving acts of God read and believed within a community, a community who confess
Jesus Christ as Lord.

Once when I was in the United States, I met with the
staff of the Y.M.C.A. in one of the big cities to discuss
with them the Christian witness of the Y.M.C.A. After
the meeting, one of the secretaries asked to drive me
back to the hotel where I was staying. On the way he
said to me, "I asked to drive you back because I wanted
to talk to you. I do not believe in most of the things
you said to us at the conference. I do not believe in

what you called the incarnation nor in redemption
through the death and resurrection of Christ." And
then he continued, "I suppose you would say that I am
not a Christian." I asked him, "What do you say you
are?" He replied, "I call myself a Christian." My answer
then was, "If you are prepared to bear the name of
Christ in a world where there are so many names which
men can bear, that is what is decisive. If you say you
are a Christian, I just accept you as one. I think your
theology is wrong and your understanding of the Christian faith meager. But that does not mean that you do
not belong to the community who bear his name."

At one of the consultations convened by the Faith
and Order Department of the World Council of
Churches, someone spoke insistently of the difference
between real Christians and nominal Christians. Archbishop Brilioth rejoined: "Surely there are only nominal Christians, those who bear the name of Christ. I
do not understand what you mean by real Christians."
When we talk of the Christian community, it is futile
to talk of one particular brand of ethics, or our particular denomination and its traditions. Speaking at the
closing meeting of the first assembly of the World
Council of Churches, Archbishop Fisher said, "We may
not like each other, but we are strangely alike."

Those who consent to bear the name of Christ belong
to the Christian family. Within this family the Bible is
read and understood. Differences of understanding and
doctrine, differences of tradition and practice, are held

within the one community. It is not a community organized by like-minded people—a kind of mutual admiration society. It is one which exists having come down through the corridors of time. God called Abraham to become the father of a people. In Jesus Christ, this people were defined by belief in his name. That is the Church.

At the International Missionary Conference held at Tambaram in 1938, I happened to be the secretary of the section that dealt with "The Authority of the Faith." After a whole day of discussion, Dr. Van Dusen, the chairman, asked everyone to come prepared the next day to state, in three sentences, the faith by which he lived. Dr. Kraemer was the first person called upon the next day to give his three sentences. Kraemer said, "I live by faith in the deeds of God. I feel nothing about them. I stand on them." Dr. Walter Horton put what he had to say into one sentence. "I live," he said, "by faith in the objective atonement of Christ."

The deeds of God—they are our standing ground; and one of these deeds is the creation of a people. We can protest, as Rousseau protested, and say, "If God wanted to get hold of me, why must he go all the way round to Abraham?" But the peculiarity of a deed is that you cannot argue about it. It is done. One might wish that it were done some other way, but that wish serves no purpose. The Church is. It has a history.

This is why it is not possible just to collect people and to make churches. The Church is a historical community which one joins. It is an identifiable group of people whose history goes back to the call of Abraham. There are, of course, Christian groups which are not churches. There was, for instance, in India a group called The Fellowship of the Friends of Jesus. These were men who accepted Jesus Christ as Lord and Savior but who refused to become members of the church through baptism. The No-Church Movement in Japan is similar in ethos. Then there are institutions like the Y.M.C.A. The point is that, when one is talking about the Church, one is talking about something that is pegged down in history, so that individual preferences and differences of opinion become necessarily subordinate in the discussion.

When I was a young minister in Ceylon, our district chairman proposed that instead of using bread and wine for Holy Communion, we should use milk and biscuits. He said that the elements used in Holy Communion in any place must be the common food in that place. It simply so happened, he said, that since Jesus was a Jew, he used bread and wine. Of course, this proposal came to nothing; for one cannot treat the fact that Jesus was a Jew as a chance event. When God decided to become man, he decided to become a Jew. It is not possible to change the elements of Holy Communion without challenging this decision of God. The Incarnation is historical event, and the fact that we use bread and wine for Holy Communion acknowledges that our faith is rooted in history.

Dr. Walter Horton said, "I live by faith in the objective atonement of Jesus Christ." The deed of God by which men are forgiven is a secular event. This is not to say that there is no experience of forgiveness outside faith in Jesus Christ. Hinduism knows a good deal of the experience of forgiveness. So does Judaism. The peculiar assertion of the Christian faith is that this experience of forgiveness, which we have as men and women, is part of and is rooted in a cosmic event. The atonement for sin wrought by and in Jesus Christ through his birth, death, and resurrection is something objective. So that truly to know one's sins forgiven is also to recognize one's involvement in God's atoning action and activity in and for the whole world. My forgiveness is part of an objective atonement.

Dr. Russel Chandran was broadcasting a message on Easter Day. He showed me his script. "The message of Easter," he said, "is that death is not the end." I asked him, "But, Chandran, did it happen? Did Jesus Christ actually rise from the dead?" His reply was, "Only the men of faith saw the risen Christ." It seems to me that this way of putting it will just not do. The Easter stories in the Gospels have a common conclusion—"Go and tell." The Easter event is an event to be proclaimed. Something has happened which can be announced and therefore must be announced. "Jesus Christ has risen from the dead." It is by faith that the risen Christ is apprehended. But the Resurrection itself is not an event of faith in Jesus Christ. It is something that happened to Jesus Christ. (Acts 2:24; Rom. 1:4.)

But this happened-ness, which is the foundation of the Christian faith, relates not only to the past but also to the future. The risen Christ is ascended and "He will come." So that when we talk about the Christian community as being pegged down in history, we are talking about it as being held between a past and a future. This situation determines the nature of the Church and its total tradition.

Let all that I have said so far be an introduction to what I want to do now, and that is to look at the three main streams of the Christian heritage, so that we may see something of the richness of the Christian community. The three streams are the Catholic, the Protestant, and the Puritan. It will be obvious that I am not here talking about denominations. Let me tell a story which may be apocryphal but which I heard about Dr. Nicholas Zernoff, a member of the Russian Orthodox Church. It is said that at a dinner one day, in England, he was sitting next to a lady whom he was meeting for the first time. By way of opening the conversation with her at dinner, he turned to her and said, "Madam, are you a Catholic or a Protestant?" She replied, "I am a Presbyterian." To which he answered, "Madam, I did not ask about your denomination, I asked you about your theology. Are you a Catholic or a Protestant?"

The three streams of the Christian heritage run within almost every denomination: so that to talk about

Catholic, Protestant, and Puritan is not to talk about denominations at all, but to talk about the three major marks of the Christian Church as a whole, all three of which are present within practically every denomination.

Of necessity, I must oversimplify the complex issues which arise in the kind of discussion on which we are about to embark. But sometimes oversimplification is the only way of seeing the issues themselves clearly.

CATHOLIC

What is Catholicism? The word "catholic" is derived from the Greek *kata,* according to, and *holos,* the whole. When white light is passed through a prism we get a spectrum: violet, indigo, blue, green, yellow, orange, red. The spectrum is catholic. It is according to the whole. In it, all the elements of white light are broken up and presented in their order and proportions. The Catholic insistence can be understood when we realize that what is insisted upon is that a church must maintain in its own life all the various elements that belong to the Christian heritage and in their due order and proportion. But are our churches catholic? Unfortunately, no. We have so broken up the Church, that some churches are violet, indigo, blue; others are yellow, orange, red; and still others are just plain purple.

Catholicism, however, is a true Christian concern.

A church must be according to the whole. Should a
Catholic be asked, "When you are concerned with
Catholicism, what is your standing ground?" I think
he would express himself something like this: "I am
concerned with the givenness of the church." When is
a church, a church? The Catholic answer would be, "A
church is a church when it is according to the whole."

The secondary meaning of the word "catholic,"
which is "universal," is dependent on its primary meaning. The Church is universal because it is catholic. It
embraces all because it is dependent on the prejudices
of none. Since the Church is defined by history, it is
neither a matter of personal taste nor of purely personal
judgment. Should people, on the basis of purely personal
judgment or likes and dislikes, come together, they
would not make a church. To attempt to make a church
is like taking a man and a woman and three children
and putting them inside a house and saying to them,
"You are a family." We do not make churches, we just
join the Church. This is what Catholicism is about.
This is what it means to say that the Church is given.

The wholeness of the Church implies, also, the wholeness of truth. If two and two do not make four, three
and three will not make six. The two facts are part of
each other. They hold together. We say that we believe
in the priesthood of all believers, but we fail often to
realize that this doctrine is false if we do not also believe in the priestly nature of the Church. The two are
true together. We say that we believe in the Church

as the body of Christ, but we do not often realize that this belief is dependent on the truth of the doctrine of election. Again the two are true together.

Now, however, we have got ourselves into the parlous condition in which the Church has been broken into churches and the wholeness of truth has been shattered. Truths which belong together are now held apart in separated denominations, so that necessity is laid on us to seek to recover wholeness. This we can do only by churches being open toward one another, and by listening to one another until they understand. Dr. Lindsay, master of Balliol College, Oxford, speaking to a philosophy class, said: "Before you can understand the teaching of any particular philosopher, you must ask and find the answer to three questions: (1) What does he say? (2) Can I agree with him? (3) Why does he, who is more intelligent than I, believe such rubbish?"

The third question is surely the most important and the most difficult to answer. Until we know the answer to this question, we do not really undertand what that particular philosopher is saying. The same is true about churches. Take the Roman Catholic doctrine of the Immaculate Conception, for instance. We Protestants find it impossible to believe it. We think it is rubbish. But how is it that our fellow Christians in the Roman Catholic Church who are, many of them, far more intelligent than we are, and at least equally honest, believe in this doctrine?

This search for the wholeness of truth is what the

ecumenical movement is about. It means that Christians who think differently and believe differently meet together and think together, until they understand one another. Oliver Tomkins, the present Bishop of Bristol, and at that time Secretary of the Faith and Order Department of the World Council of Churches, once explained his work by saying: "I am like a boxing promoter. The work of my department is to bring the churches together into the same boxing ring and then to see that no one runs away."

Let us look at this position that the Church is given also from another point of view. Again and again in church union discussion, the question has to be faced, "If the Church is given and has come down to us through history, what are the marks of its continuity?" No one disputes the significance of this question, because all churches are Catholic at this point. They only give different answers to the question that is raised. They do not agree among themselves as to what the organs of continuity are.

The Salvation Army would say that "the faith" is the sufficient organ of continuity. And by this they mean the faith which is given to us in Holy Scripture. The Congregationalists would say that this answer is not enough. They would add to it an insistence on the sacraments. But the Methodists would say that faith and sacraments as organs of continuity are not enough. To these must be added the ministry. The Anglicans would say it is not enough to talk simply of the ministry. The ministry must be the threefold order of bishop, presbyter, and deacon, with the bishop being in the historic episcopate. The Orthodox would say that the historic episcopate by itself will not do. The episcopate must be tied, in its consecration and in its function, to the holy liturgy. The Roman Catholics would say that even this will no do. The episcopate must be based upon the primacy of Peter. Complex and confusing as all this argument may be, yet the basic issue is important—continuity in space and time is an essential quality of the Church.

To repeat then, the Church is given, and the Catholic is right in his insistence on the givenness of the Church.

PROTESTANT

What is the Protestant emphasis? Just as the concern of the Catholic is with the givenness of the Church, the concern of the Protestant is with the sovereignty of God. The battle cry of the Reformation was *Sola-Gratia, Sola-Fide*. The qualification "alone" was dictated by the concern that man should not seek to enmesh God in religion or morality. In an address which I was giving one day in a church in the United States, I said in the course of my speech, "Let us take, for instance, a Roman Catholic and a Quaker . . . ," and then I stopped. I said: "That won't do because they are too much alike; let us rather look at a Roman Catholic

and a Presbyterian," and so I went on. At the end of the
meeting, after I had gone to my room, there was a
knock at the door. The minister of the church where I
was speaking had come to see me. He said: "I want to
ask you a question. You spoke about Roman Catholics
and Quakers being alike, but I cannot for the life of me
find anything in common between them. What did you
mean?" I explained to him that there was one particular matter in which Roman Catholics and Quakers
resembled each other. Both groups were sure about
God. The Catholics claimed to possess the Christian
tradition in its wholeness. The Quakers claimed to
possess the Inner Light. The Presbyterians, on the
other hand, held at the center of their faith, the assertion
that under no circumstance can God be made man's
possession. The mystery of the sovereignty of God per-
vades every aspect of Presbyterianism.

Whether Luther or Calvin, both were concerned to
maintain that salvation was by grace alone, because it
was the grace of a sovereign God. God remained
sovereign even in his exercise of grace. Also it was because grace was grace alone that the Church, while it
was given in and through history, remained in constant
need of reformation. "Reformed and always reforming"
is the only context in which it is possible to take the
givenness of the Church seriously.

Nowhere is the unprotestant nature of our denominations more clear than in church union discussions.
How easily, around the negotiating table, do we speak

of the churches as if they were our churches! We turn
God's light into our enlightenment, God's gifts into our
heritage, God's grace into our experience, God's faithfulness into our traditions. Scripture says that there is
only one way of making ours that which belongs to
God. The husbandmen in the parable said, "This is
the son; let us kill him and then the vineyard will be
ours." (Matt. 21:38.)

Our heritage is not ours. It belongs to God and must
remain at God's disposal. That God can raise up children for Abraham out of stones is not simply a warning. It is also a promise—a promise to the world. The
whole of church history abounds with examples of those
whom God raised up to do his will and to carry his
message—men and women who are evidence that God
remains sovereign over the Church and over the world.

It must be evident, then, that the Catholic and
Protestant emphases belong together. The Catholic
concern by itself can immobilize the Church and make
it captive to history; while the Protestant emphasis by
itself can be fissiparous in its results. The Protestant
affirmation *Sola Scriptura* does not mean that Scripture
stands alone, but that Scripture alone is the standing
ground of the Christian community. Scripture is about
the saving acts of God, read and believed within a community who confess Jesus Christ. The very word Protestant derives from the Latin *protestare,* which means
"to confess." To be a Protestant is to confess that God in
Jesus Christ remains sovereign.

The opposite of a Catholic is a sectarian. To be a sectarian is to remain unconcerned about the wholeness of the life of the Christian family. The sectarian approach to church union, for instance, is "Why worry? The Church is invisible. And as far as the visible churches are concerned, they represent no challenge to faith." As for the word Protestant, the nearest that I can think of to describe its opposite is the word religious. In its general use, religion is the result of man's attempt to make God serve human need. The essential emphasis of the Protestant faith is that man must serve God's purposes. In Jesus Christ, these purposes of God for the world were declared.

PURITAN

The Church is Catholic—it must be Catholic. The Church is Protestant—it must be Protestant. The Church is also Puritan.

What is the Puritan emphasis? The Puritan insists on the distinguishability of the Christian community, the identifiability of the Christian witness. Scripture speaks of God's people as a pilgrim people whose life in the world will, therefore, be characterized by the fact that they are a people on the move. Scripture speaks, too, of God's people as a soldiering people who will not, therefore, be entangled in civilian pursuits. And again Scripture speaks of God's people as a separated people who, in the midst of a common life, live also a life which is peculiarly their own.

The characteristic word in the Puritan tradition is "discipline." There is the discipline involved because of who we are, because of the task in which we are engaged, and because of the goal toward which we are moving. It is a tragedy that, in the ecumenical movement today, the Puritan voice is largely silent. This is because, on the one hand, many who would call themselves Puritans hold themselves aloof from the ecumenical fellowship, in the name of a moralism which is itself a denial of what Puritanism is about; while, on the other hand, those who are within the ecumenical fellowship do not yet seem to have found a way of expressing their concern which would elicit attention.

My purpose here cannot be to deal with this subject of discipline with any exhaustiveness, but to show by simple illustrations what the nature of the issue is. I said that there is the discipline which is the result of who we are. This means many things. First, there are those disciplines which I undertake for myself because I know what kind of person I am, and what the disciplines are which I need. It is said of Jesus that it was his custom to go to the synagogue every Sabbath morning. That was part of his discipline. I have a friend who gives to some other family the same amount of money that he spends on presents for his children at Christmas. That is part of his discipline. The issues here are never wholly issues as between right and wrong.

Secondly, there is the discipline necessary because I know something about my neighbor. I had a friend who became a drunkard. His wife and children had a miserable time. I went to him one day to speak with him about this. He said to me: "The first time I was offered a drink at a social function, I refused it. Later on, I went to a friend of mine who was a layman and a lay preacher in the church, a very good man and a very saintly man. I asked him whether it was wrong to drink. He said to me, 'No, as long as you drink in moderation. I, too, take drinks at social functions.' " My friend said: "I took his word and began to drink at social functions. This is now the result." What went wrong here in the case of my friend was that he posed the question in terms of right and wrong and got an answer in those terms. Neither he nor his friend who advised him looked at the problem in terms of disciplined living, recognizing the kind of people they were.

I have also said that there is the discipline involved because of the nature of our work. The normal diet in Ashrams in India is vegetarian. Celibacy in the Christian ministry is also very much a question of what the task demands. A new issue that is arising in this connection is how we can get long-term missionaries to work in the lands of Asia and Africa unless they are celibates. In Asia and Africa the problems of children's education is, for Westerners, quickly becoming an insoluble one.

I have also said that there is a discipline involved

because of the goal toward which we are moving. Let one example suffice to illustrate this. We are moving toward the goal of a united Church. If this is true, it is essential that we should already discipline ourselves to eat in each other's houses and to enjoy the food in each other's homes. I am a Methodist and enjoy the Methodist way of worship. The first time that I went to worship in an Orthodox church, I did not enjoy it at all. But I must stay with it until I do enjoy it. It is not that I shall ever like it as much as what has been my own. But I must like it nevertheless. When I am traveling in the West and have been worshiping in English, or some other language, for a long time, I get restless. I have to go out into the woods somewhere and sing some Tamil lyrics before I find my spiritual balance again. Differences in the food there will always be, and preferences with respect to food; but it is part of the discipline imposed by where we are going that we should learn to worship in each other's ways. The same is true of methods of Bible study, and so on.

The examples which I have given have been chosen specifically with the intention of showing what it means to speak about discipline without raising the question of right and wrong. But once this approach is clear, the essential questions as to what should constitute the disciplines of the Christian community, as a community in the world, remain. There are the disciplined communities within the Church like the religious orders, the friars, and the like. But there must also be that which characterizes the Church as a whole and makes it identifiable in the world as a community under discipline. It is here that a great deal of new thinking is necessary. Indeed, the churches of Asia and Africa are, in a greater sense, communities with a discipline than are the older churches of the West.

Let me bring this whole discussion to a close by insisting that the Church has to be all three—Catholic, Protestant, and Puritan. It is inevitable that within the Church, some of us would have the Catholic concern as determinative in our thinking and living; others of us, the Protestant concern; and still others, the Puritan concern. But the Church as a whole has to be all three. Indeed, within every church, there are all three. Speaking as a Methodist, I would point out, within The Methodist Church, the Protestant emphasis which largely stems from John Wesley, the Catholic emphasis enshrined in the hymns of Charles Wesley, and the Puritan emphasis which belongs to the tradition that goes back to George Whitefield and Bishop Asbury. In the Roman Catholic Church one finds the Augustinian tradition which is Protestant, the Thomist tradition which is Catholic, and the Franciscan tradition which is Puritan. I know that to use names of persons in this way is not quite correct, but I have done it to illustrate a fact which is certainly significant. The three traditions belong together. It is in the wholeness of the Church that the integrity of the Church lies.

CHAPTER 6

WHY DIVIDE OUR HERITAGE?

In the last chapter we considered the nature of the Church's heritage and the importance of the three traditions within it—Catholic, Protestant, and Puritan. In this chapter we shall carry this discussion forward and consider the richness and variety of the traditions within the Church from a more personal point of view: that is, by considering the different ways in which men appropriate the gospel. But even before I do this, I want to narrate two incidents that concern myself which tell their own story. In a sense they will serve as an introduction to the personal nature of this whole discussion.

When I wrote my book *Upon the Earth,* its first draft, in manuscript form, was submitted for criticism to a commission of nearly thirty-five theologians belonging to various churches, which was set up by the World Council of Churches. It was, for me, an interesting experience to participate in this discussion when, day after day, my book was criticized, chapter by chapter. At one point in the discussion, there was quite serious criticism by Bishop Hollis and Bishop Newbigin of my doctrine of the Holy Spirit. As the discussion was proceeding, Colin Williams, who was in the chair, said to Bishop Newbigin: "When you say that you disagree with Niles on this point, all you are saying is that you

are not a Methodist. That is what Bishop Hollis is saying too. In spite of the personal nuance, Niles is simply
explaining Methodist teaching on the Holy Spirit." I
myself was not aware that I was being such a good
Methodist. The point that I am trying to make is that,
having been reared in a Methodist home, having grown
up in the Methodist Church, and having in my own
personal life been nourished by the hymns of Charles
Wesley, Methodism had become part of me. It was in
my blood and bones.

Let me, in an aside, say here that I have always found
it difficult to understand the fears that people entertain
that, when church union comes, their particular tradition might be overwhelmed or lost. When we go into a
united Church, we go with our traditions as part of
ourselves, and they cannot get lost.

Let me now speak of the other incident which, as it
were, is a footnote to what I have been saying. I was
speaking at a united public meeting in Middles-
borough, England, the chairman of which was Archbishop William Temple, at that time Archbishop of
York. At the close of the meeting he came up to me and
said, "Niles, to what church do you belong?" I told
him I was a Methodist. His eyes twinkled and he said to
me, "You don't even smell like a Methodist." I did not
ask him how Methodists smell!

When we live within the heritage of the whole
Church, we shall find that there are two things which
are simultaneously true. First, we shall have our own

standing ground. Each one of us has his own home. None of us can be the whole thing. But secondly and at the same time, we shall be aware that we live in a house which is much bigger than the rooms we occupy.

Let me leave it at that and now seek to elucidate the question with which I wanted to deal in this chapter: that is, the various ways in which men appropriate the gospel and witness to their experience of salvation.

The second World Conference of Christian Youth was held in 1947 at Oslo. The assembly hall of the conference belonged to the Pentecostal Church. The day before the conference opened, Oliver Tomkins (now Bishop of Bristol) and I were walking down the road to the conference office. A man was standing on a ladder, cleaning the windows of the conference hall. He turned and saw us and, clambering down the ladder, he took Oliver's hands and asked him, "Brother, are you saved?" Oliver, taken aback by the question, stammered, "Yes." The man said, "Praise the Lord," and went back to his window cleaning. When I got to the office, I told Dr. Visser t' Hooft, the General Secretary of the World Council of Churches, what had happened. He said to me, "If I had been in Oliver's place, I would not have said, 'Yes.' I would have said, 'Yes, in hope.' "

Let us look at this answer. Why did Visser t' Hooft insist that he would never have said, "Yes," but only, "Yes, in hope"? It was because that was the way the Bible talked about it. Paul speaks of the word of the cross as the power of God "to us who are being saved" (1 Cor. 1:18). Writing to Titus, he says, "He saved us so that we might be justified by his grace and become heirs in hope of eternal life." (Tit. 3:5-7.) In other words, to be saved is to be in a process of salvation. It is to be set on a course. It is to be upheld by hope of something yet to happen. Or as Paul puts it, stating it from the human end, "I press on to apprehend that for which I was apprehended" (Phil. 3:12).

We do not know when Paul was apprehended by Jesus Christ. All we know is that story of Saul of Tarsus on the Damascus road, where Jesus met him and told him that he was already apprehended, that he was already yoked, that already the crossbeam with the pricks was in place behind the plow, and that should Saul kick, he would simply get hurt. To be saved was to be apprehended by Christ and be set by him toward a hope. Again, to quote the words of Paul, "Him, which is Christ in you the hope of glory, we proclaim, warning every man and teaching every man in all wisdom that we may present every man mature in Christ." (Col. 1:27-28.) No wonder that, writing to the Corinthians, Paul says, "I buffet my body and bring it under bondage, lest having preached to others, I myself should be damned." (I Cor. 9:27.) Can we not then imagine someone saying to Paul, "Brother, are you saved?" and Paul answering, "Yes, in hope; I press on, lest I be damned."

Let us use two passages from John also to illuminate

this truth. There is first of all the great text in John 3:16—"God so loved the world." As we can see from the context, the emphasis is on the new possibility that has been opened up for men to participate in the love of God for the world. In that God has become man in Jesus Christ, men can now so attach themselves to him by faith, that instead of being useless, even as anything that has perished is useless, they can be useful to him in the life which he lives in the world. That life alone is eternal life. In that life we can now share.

Or, as we read in the story of Nicodemus (John 3: 1-15), the way to the new birth is to take one's stand where the new is happening. It is like standing where the winds blow, so that they blow on your face: or, to change the metaphor, it is like standing where the fires are burning, so that a spark may fall on your heart. There is no use in closing the doors and windows of the church and then keeping the electric fans going, circulating the hot air. The question "Are you saved?" can be answered only by a church and in a church where the doors and windows are open to the world. It is a question about the saving activity of God and not simply about oneself. So we answer, "Yes, in hope." God has put a song into my heart and a message upon my lips and a work into my hands and has said to me, "Work out your own salvation, for it is I who work in you, both to will and to work my good pleasure" (Phil. 2:13).

Some months after this incident in Oslo, I was having

a long conversation with Pastor Pierre Maury. He was the head of the Reformed Church of France, and, in my own personal experience, one of the humblest, saintliest, and wisest men that I had ever known. I told Pierre of the incident at Oslo and the answer that Visser t'Hooft told me he would have given. Pierre said to me, "If I were asked the question 'Are you saved?' I would not give the answer that Visser t'Hooft gave. I would say, 'I do not know. But one thing I know—Jesus Christ is my Savior.' "

Why did Pierre Maury insist on such a different answer? Because, once again, he was taking his stand upon Scripture. The confession of a Christian cannot be about himself. It can only be about his Lord. In any case, there is very little about me which I know. Psychologists tell me that seven eighths of me is underground, and that I can hardly know much about it. Even about the one eighth which is above ground, I know very little. In fact, I know more about Jesus Christ than I know about myself. If it were a question about him, I could answer it. He is the Savior; he is my Savior and yours. But about myself, I do not know what to say. I believe in him, but I do not know whether I really believe in him or not. I have repented, but I do not know how deep or sincere is my repentance. I follow him, but I do not know to what extent it is he that I am following. Whenever I think about myself, I am lost in a psychological tangle, so that if I am asked, "Are you saved?" I can only answer, "I do not know." But one thing I do know—Jesus Christ is my Savior. He knows me. He made me. He loves me. And if I am saved, it is because he keeps me safe.

At the Assembly of the World Council of Churches held at Evanston in 1954, a message was put out. It was, I think, the only occasion at a big Christian gathering when the general message was passed by a majority vote. One of the main figures in the opposition to the text of the message was Pierre Maury. Some months after Evanston, I was speaking to him about this incident and asked him why he voted against that message. He said to me: "That message was a message to the world. It was a message to men, many of whom do not believe in Jesus Christ. When you are talking to that kind of person, there is only one thing you have to tell him, and that is that God loves him. The Evanston message was too involved theologically and too heavy on the note of judgment."

Was Pierre Maury right? I think he was. It is far more important to tell a man, "God loves you," than to ask him, "Do you love God?" It is far more important to tell him, "God believes in you," than to ask him, "Do you believe in God?" It is far more important to tell him, "Jesus Christ is your Savior," than to ask him, "Are you saved?" As Pierre Maury said to me, when you get hold of that poor fellow who is a drunkard or that poor woman who is an unmarried mother, just tell that person, "My brother (my sister),

God loves you, God believes in you, in Jesus Christ and because of Jesus Christ."

Let me put the matter in another way. We must live and teach men and women to live in the passive voice. That is the way to live abundantly. That is, for instance, the characteristic of a true home. At home, I live as a person who is loved by my wife and by my children. My family is conscious of the same feeling. The children do not get up in the morning and say, "We must today love father and mother." They simply live as those who are loved. Should the atmosphere of the home become an atmosphere in the active voice, everybody in it would soon be living on their nerves. Men and women need to learn that they can live in the passive voice, that they can live as those who have been loved, as those who have been loved together in Jesus Christ. Indeed, in John's epistle, the active voice is derived from the passive voice. "He has loved us together, therefore let us love one another." (I John 4:11.)

In this conversation that I had with Pierre Maury, I also asked him about the universalistic implication of saying, simply and without qualification, "Jesus Christ is my Savior and yours." Pierre replied by pointing out one difference between the way in which the parable of the lost sheep is given in Matthew's Gospel and the way it is given in Luke's Gospel. In Luke's Gospel, the shepherd says, "I will go and seek my sheep until I find it." There is no question but that the sheep is found. In Matthew's Gospel, the shepherd goes out to seek his sheep, "if so be that he find it." There is the chance that the sheep may be lost. (Luke 15:4-7; Matt. 18:12-13.) Pierre said to me, "Whenever you think of yourself, think of the parable in Matthew's Gospel; but whenever you are thinking about somebody else, think of the parable in Luke's Gospel." How right he was! Our natural tendency is to have it the other way round. It is about ourselves that we are sure. It is about our neighbor that we seem to have doubts!

In all our thinking, we must make God's love for men in Jesus Christ our standing ground. When Paul said, "Nothing can separate us from the love of God in Christ Jesus our Lord" (Rom. 8:39), he was not talking about our love toward God. He was not saying that we should love him in life or in death. He was saying, rather, that God's love for us was something which no circumstance of life could stop or alter. He loves all the time. As Frederick W. H. Myers puts it in his poem, "Saint Paul":

Christ, I am Christ's and let the name suffice you;
　Aye, for me, too, it greatly hath sufficed.
Lo, with no winning words would I entice you,
　Paul has no honor and no friend but Christ.

Yea, through life, death, through sorrow and through sinning,
　Christ shall suffice me, for He hath sufficed;

Christ is the end, for Christ was the beginning,
  Christ the beginning, for the end is Christ.

But this business of talking about Jesus Christ and his love is and can be very difficult. One cannot commend the love of the Savior except by loving. Words by themselves will carry no conviction.

Pierre Maury knew better than anybody else that words will not say it. I love to think of the way in which Pierre Maury died. He went to Madagascar and Algeria during the period of war and tension between France and these lands. He sat down with the people there, man by man, and listened to their stories of war and their suffering. Anybody who knew Pierre would know how he must have carried the burdens of these people on his soul and prayed for them. Actually, the experience proved too much for him. He was old and not physically strong. He came back to France, and the next day he lay on his bed and died. That is the way to say, "Jesus loves you!" That is the only way of speaking to which the world will listen. We talk too much about ourselves. We must learn to talk about Christ. And as Pierre Maury would say, "to talk about him alone."

Sometime after my conversation with Pierre Maury, I had the opportunity to pay a visit to Karl Barth in Basel. In my conversation with him, I told him about my discussion of the question of salvation with both his friends, Visser t' Hooft and Pierre Maury. I asked him, "Dr. Barth, suppose I should put the same question to you, 'Are you saved?' how would you answer it?" He replied, "If you had asked me this question about fifteen years ago, I would have given you either the answer of Pierre Maury or of Visser t' Hooft. Today, I would simply say, 'Yes.' "

What is the basis of that simple answer? Again, Holy Scripture. When Paul and Silas were imprisoned in Philippi, there was a sudden earthquake. The jailer, who had been asleep, got up with a start to find all the doors and windows open. He was not sure what had happened, but it seemed certain that the prisoners had escaped. What would he tell the magistrates in the morning? He certainly would lose his job. He might possibly lose his life. So he pulled out his sword to commit suicide. Paul shouted to him and said, "Do yourself no harm, for we are all here." When the jailer heard Paul's voice, he rushed to Paul and said, "What must I do to be safe?" Paul's answer was, "I cannot tell you what you must do to be safe—safe from what the magistrates may do to you. But one thing I know, if you commit your life to Jesus Christ, you will be safe whatever happens—safe in this life and the next, and not only safe yourself but also your wife and children." (Acts 16:25.)

To the question "Are you safe?" I can answer: "Yes. He who called me is faithful. He who began will finish. And, already I know, because the Holy Spirit has taught me to say, Abba—Father." (Rom. 8:15; Phil. 1:6; Thess. 5:24.)

In the second letter to Timothy, there is a scripture which puts this assurance into unmistakable language. "I know in whom I have believed, and I am persuaded that he will keep that which I have committed to him against that day." (II Tim. 1:12.) God said to me, "Will you?" and I said, "Yes." This "Yes" is in his keeping. I have committed it to him. He will keep it against that day. If I fall, he will raise me; if I weaken, he will strengthen me; if I sin, he will forgive me; if I am wayward, he will discipline me; if I am rebellious, he will chastise me. But one thing he will not do, he will not leave me. So that to the question "Are you saved?" I have only one answer, "Yes, I know I am safe."

There are different ways in which men appropriate the riches of the gospel. All the three answers we have been thinking about are scriptural answers. Each reflects a way in which men come to know and participate in the redemption of Christ and in the faithfulness of God, a way in which they come to acknowledge the lordship of Christ and share in his mission to the world.

Let me close by calling attention to an issue which belongs inevitably to this question about salvation— the issue that there is always a "now" implied in the question "Are you saved?" "Now is the day of salvation.

Today if you should hear his voice, harden not your hearts." (Heb. 3:12-14.)

We must reckon with this "now," for in the decisions that we shall have to make, there will not merely be choice between that which is prudent and that which is foolish, between that which is efficient and that which is ineffective, but also decisions between that which is obedient and that which is disobedient. We cannot pick and choose the time when ultimate decisions force themselves upon us. And inside every "now" the issue of salvation lies hidden. It cannot be sidestepped or overlooked.

CHAPTER 7

WHITHER ARE WE BOUND?

It seems only right that we should take, as our last theme, the basis on which our hopes are built. I have entitled this chapter "Whither are we bound?"—not because I want to speak about the goal of the Christian mission but rather because I want to speak about the ground on which we seek constantly to strive toward that goal. I have also chosen a text which seemed to me to point to where our eyes must turn as we come to the close of this discussion.

"I will make the valley of Achor a door of hope, says the Lord." (Hos. 2:15.)

At the beginning of the Old Testament story, and just when Israel had entered the Promised Land, there is recorded a very disturbing incident. Israel had been defeated at the Battle of Ai, and Joshua found that this defeat stemmed from the duplicity of Achan. Therefore, Achan and all who belonged to him were stoned to death in the valley of Achor. (Josh. 7:24-25.) A similar incident is recorded at the beginning of the New Testament story just when the Church was launched upon its mission. Ananias and Sapphira were caught in an act of dishonesty and struck dead. (Acts 5:5.) The significance of these two incidents lies in the witness they bear to one essential truth. That which belongs to God is God's, and God will not allow himself to be defrauded.

When God gives to Israel the sign of the Valley of Achor as their door of hope, he is saying to them, "You are mine and I will keep my own. I shall not be defrauded." In all our life and work this is the final basis of our hope, that God remains God whatever happens and that he will keep his own. As we come to the end of this study, we shall do well to take our stand on this assurance. The work is his; we are his; they are his; the future is his; and these which belong to God will remain God's.

THE WORK IS HIS

The charter of all Christian work is that God himself is the Workman. The words of Jesus were, "My Father worketh and I work. What the Father has given me to do, I do in like manner." (John 5:17-19.) Our situation is not simply that we are working for God, but that we are working with him in a world in which he himself is at work.

One of the constant themes in the book of Psalms is this fact concerning the determining character of God's working in the world:

> The nations rage, the kingdoms totter;
> He utters his voice, the earth melts.
> Come, behold the works of the Lord,
> How he has wrought desolations in the earth.

Unless the Lord builds the house,
Those who build it labour in vain.
Unless the Lord watches over the city,
The watchman stays awake in vain.

(Ps. 46:6, 8; 127:1.)

This constant activity of God constitutes the texture of human history, and by it is determined the ultimate outcome and significance of the things which men do. For instance, there is no doubt that God is working for the freedom of Africa and its peoples. Men are working too. But every time men get what can be called freedom, it does not necessarily mean that they have got what God intends. Men have a tendency to absolutize their goals. It is freedom they want. But in the last analysis, what God wants is Africa. So that no achievement of human freedom can remain a sure possession, until it becomes part of the larger purposes of God.

We are always in this kind of dilemma, so that there is nothing that can really sustain us in our work and striving except our recognition of the fact that ultimately the work is his and that he remains God.

The implication of this truth which we are trying to grasp can be made clear by reference to another biblical incident. God promised Abraham that he would have a son. For ten years Abraham and Sarah waited, until Abraham was a hundred years old, and yet they had no

son. In this circumstance it was natural to think that
they had misunderstood what God intended. "Take
Hagar," Sarah said to Abraham. "That is probably
what God meant." When Ishmael was born, Abraham
set the baby before the Lord and asked for his blessing.
But God said to Abraham, "This is not what I meant.
You have made a mistake." Abraham cried out to God
in his dilemma, "But what am I to do now? What do
I do with Ishmael?" God's answer to Abraham was one
of the most comforting of answers, "I shall be with
Ishmael also" (Gen. 16, 17). We serve a God with
whom we can trust our mistakes. Our Isaac is his, our
Ishmael is also his.

There we must leave it, learning from God to depend
on him that our work with him and for him may be
relieved of all its anxiety. "You cannot open the bud
into a blossom; He who does it does it so simply."

WE ARE HIS

The assurance that God may not be defrauded carries
no greater weight anywhere else than it carries here.
It comes with tremendous comfort to the individual.
In the high priestly prayer of Jesus it finds expression
in memorable words: "I have kept those whom you
gave me and no one was lost except the son of loss"
(John 17:12).

The mystery of Judas must remain a mystery, and
any attempt to get rid of it, either by a false universal-

ism or a flat immanentism, is unscriptural. But over against that mystery as a background, we affirm, as Paul affirmed, that we are his because he chose us. "He set me apart before I was born," says Paul. "I was apprehended by him." (Gal. 1:15; Phil. 3:12.)

Often we put so much stress on our decision for Christ that we forget the overriding importance of his decision about us. I was his before he became mine. In one of the agonizing conversations between God and Jeremiah, Jeremiah asks God, "When did you really get hold of me?" and God answers, "When you were still in your mother's womb" (Jer. 1:5). We are his, and he will not be defrauded.

In the play *The House by the Stable,* by Charles Williams, there is an episode in which Hell and Pride have got Man drunk and have persuaded him to gamble for his soul. But, even so, Man is drunkenly responsive to the call of God, a response which God is quick to meet with grace. Seeing this, Hell exclaims in disgust, "Damn him, who thought grace was so near as to hear that small squeak of a drunken voice."

Yes, grace is always near; and nearest when man seems farthest away. It is appropriate that, in the first occurrence in Scripture where grace is the theme, it is associated with a man like Noah, about whom we have only one personal story, and that a story about his drunkenness. (Gen. 9:8-24.) God's grace toward man is more than undeserved; it is God meeting man when

man is hardly conscious of himself or of his relation
to God.

THEY ARE HIS

The work is his. We are his. They also are his. Who
are *they?* If you are a white in South Africa, the black
is his. If you are black in South Africa, the white is
his. If you are an African, the English, the Belgian,
the French, and the Portuguese are his. If you are a
member of the government, the member of the opposition is his. "They are his," whoever they are.

The prophet Amos has an outstanding thing to say:
"He who brought Israel from Egypt," he affirms, "also
brought the Philistines from Caphtor and the Syrians
from Kir" (Amos 9:7). Philistia and Syria were the
enemies of Israel, but they too were his. The Hebrews
crossed the Red Sea and walked into a new land; the
Egyptians lost their king and their firstborn and now
faced a new day. Deliverance was deliverance for both.

The truth of God in Christ is truth for all men,
because it is truth about all men. It is because Jesus is
the truth about you that you have to make up your
mind about Jesus. If any man could leave Jesus alone,
he need not decide about him.

This all-embracing nature of the Christian faith,
however, loses its evangelistic thrust when we who
know it do not live by it. It is not enough to believe
in it; it must be broken down into relevant action and

utterance. In 1940, when the S.C.M. Quadrennial Conference of India, Burma, and Ceylon was held in Ceylon, one of the jokes of the conference was the story about an Indian delegate and his journey to Ceylon. In India the train stops during mealtimes at selected stations and the passengers rush to the restaurant to take a quick meal. This particular delegate had with him a ten-rupee note. At the end of every meal he pulled out this note. But there was no time to change it. So someone else of the party paid for the meal. Finally he arrived at the conference with his ten-rupee note intact.

There are many Christians like this. "I believe in God the Father" is a ten-rupee note. It must be broken down into small change. Otherwise it is useless in one's dealings with his fellowmen. "I believe in the Holy Catholic Church" is also a ten-rupee note, but unless it is broken down into small change, this belief does not help. Somebody else will have to pay for food on the journey.

They are his whoever they are, and we carry the responsibility to make this truth known, understood, and accepted.

THE FUTURE IS HIS

Finally, the Valley of Achor is the sign to us that the future is his. The result of the working of grace in the individual is true also for all history. Because of grace, heaven and earth meet; and when they meet, heaven takes earthly form. History is the "in-timing" of God's eternal Word. "In the beginning was the Word and the Word was face to face with God and the Word became flesh." (John 1:1, 14.) God going out from himself, and in going out remaining one with himself—that is what history is. It is the Word which proceeds from God and returns to him.

But how are we sure that it will so return? We are sure because it has returned already: "The third day He rose from the dead; he ascended into heaven and sitteth at the right hand of God the Father Almighty, from thence he shall come." There is one future tense in the Church's creed, and it is a future tense about him. "He will come."

Into this future, which is where we are bound, God calls us. No analysis of all that has happened in the past, nor of the present situation, can take the place of adventure with him into that future into which he is calling us. "Watchman, what of the night? The morning comes and also the night." (Isa. 21:11, 12.) Yes, it is still night, and there is more of the night to come; but it is the night before the morning breaks, the darkness before the dawn.

The promise of Jesus to his Church was that the gates of hell shall not prevail against it. (Matt. 16:18.) The correct posture for the Church is the posture of attack. A church seeking to safeguard itself is never safe. But to the church that attacks the forms of hell, the promise

is given that the gates of hell shall not prevail. Here is
our task and our assurance.

"I give you the valley of Achor as the door of hope."

"The kingdoms of the world are become the kingdom of our God and of his Christ." (Rev. 11:15.)